THE DIFFERENCE
PLACE MAKES

THE DIFFERENCE PLACE MAKES:

Gender, Sexuality, and Diaspora Identity

Angeletta KM Gourdine

The Ohio State University Press
Columbus

Library of Congress Cataloging-in-Publication Data

Gourdine, Angeletta K. M., 1968–
  The difference place makes : gender, sexuality, and diaspora
identity / Angeletta K.M. Gourdine.
     p. cm.
  Includes bibliographical references and index.
  ISBN 0-8142-0926-2 (alk. paper) — ISBN 0-8142-5106-4 (pbk.
: alk. paper)
  1. Cliff, Michelle—Criticism and interpretation. 2. Aidoo, Ama
Ata, 1942-   —Criticism and interpretation. 3. Walker, Alice,
1944-   —Criticism and interpretation. 4. Caribbean fiction (English)—African influences. 5. American fiction—African influences.
6. Women and literature—Caribbean Area. 7. Women and literature—United States. 8. Place (Philosophy) in literature. 9. Women and literature—Ghana. 10. Women, Black, in literature.
11. Sex role in literature. 12. Exiles in literature. 13. Race in
literature.   I. Title.
PR9265.9.C55Z68 2002
813.009'9729—dc21

2002013506

Cover design by Dan O'Dair
Printed by Thomson-Shore, Inc.

The paper used in this publication meets the minimum requirements
of the American National Standard for Information Sciences—
Permanence of Paper for Printed Library Materials. ANSI Z39.48-1992.

9 8 7 6 5 4 3 2 1

for Vashti Alexandra

contents

preface

If'en you don' kno whe you gwine you should kno whe you cum
f'um
    —Gullah proverb

The Difference Place Makes speaks to the relationship between present and past locations: the geographical spaces we occupy, the cultural borders within which we place ourselves, and the intellectual positions we take. By "we" I mean people of African descent, and the borders we cross are those constructed by diasporization, which requires that we hear each other and speak across the "vagaries of our respective conditions" (Busia 2). This book "hear[s] those words whispered over the void," utterances that present "narratives of loss, exile, [and] journeying" (Busia 2; Gilroy, *Black Atlantic* 198). Diaspora invokes images of bodies and acts of movements. The dispersal of Africans from the continent resulted in the presence of African bodies in non-African places. These Africans eventually claimed their new homelands and developed cultures of resistance and subsistence. However, their gaze has remained focused on the original "nodal point" (Gilroy, *Black Atlantic* 198), the mythic place in their social history. In *The Difference Place Makes,* I contemplate the location of my body within the vast diaspora landscape, untangle ambiguities about how to represent the kinship that diaspora implies, and question what privileges membership in the diaspora grants us as we tell new tales.

I have never claimed to be anyone other than a black woman. So, when the shift to "African American" was called for by Ramona Edelin and decreed by Jesse Jackson, I was confused. After many people that I loved and respected began to name and dress themselves African American, I wondered why I felt no such need to proclaim myself an African (living on) American (soil). Many suggested that my closeness to European Americans and their ways of Being explained my rejection of even an adjectival connection to Africa. In the face of such a painful challenge, I grew reticent, knowing that my reluctance to proclaim myself African American came from my feeling that I was not African—at least not in the way that Ama Ata Aidoo and Buchi Emecheta are.

As I worked through this conundrum, I realized that my unyielding commitment to "black" was connected to my own sense of place and my relationship with my home place. As a linguist, I understood the logic of the semantic shift; it both reflects past cultural history and acknowledges current location. Still, I could not embrace the identity for myself. Then I read Soyinka's pronouncement about negritude: "A tiger does not proclaim its tigritude. He pounces" (qtd. in Jahn, *History* 265). I came to understand and appreciate the ways in which growing up in a Gullah-inflected world positioned me within the matrices of the diaspora and black studies. Soyinka explains that "the tiger does not stand in the forest and say 'I am a tiger,'" yet when we pass where a tiger has previously been, we nonetheless "know that some tigritude has been emanated there" (qtd. in Jahn, *History* 266). In this context, identity, then, is manifest in the life work(s) of a person, not in their self-proclamations.

Like the writers I discuss, I, too, am situated in a specific space, the cultural borders of Charleston, South Carolina, most significant as the principal port of entry for Africans into the British New World. Indeed, at this moment Charleston city officials and community members are negotiating the establishment of a History of Slavery Museum, to be the largest of its kind in the world. As a black girl growing up in Charleston—the bastion of Southern culture and history and an untapped vessel of living black history and culture—my great-grandmother, informed by Gullah sensibilities, made sure I knew from where I had come.

In my family, Gullah was a talk and a people. Although our peoples migrated from the islands long ago, Gullah ways remained with us, and I was educated in the Gullah tradition. The people of the Sea Islands had the climatological and geographical fortune of living in almost total isolation from Europeans. This limited contact allowed them to preserve important aspects of their African cultures.[1] In the Sea Islands, the African descendants outnumbered whites, some slaves surrogating as master on plantations for absent landowners. The experiences of the Gullah, their islands originally settled by Barbadian and other Caribbean planters as early as 1520, link them not only to the West African rice coast but also to the islands of the Caribbean. Indeed, the lilt in our voices often inspires people to ask if we are from one of the Caribbean islands.

Ebony's African American Pictorial Encyclopedia provided me with my history, so I knew who W. E. B. Du Bois was long before I could actually read his *Souls,* and I understood that the struggle on the continent for freedom was not unlike abolition. As an academic I came to understand my precarious history and how it informed the work that I do. As a living diaspora culture, the Gullah provides a mooring for me. In my family, we never openly referred to ourselves as Africans in America. Nevertheless, we had many narratives that included that history. We took them in and used them to move forward in a way that honored the courage of our ancestors. We also understood the legacy of those experiences, and in our growth into a new people, different from but connected to our ancestors, we honored them. Culturally, I am a black person, and that identity comes with an unadulterated sense of pride. Like Soyinka's metaphorical tiger, I just am.

The Difference Place Makes reflects my engagement with my diaspora sisters, an attempt to reconsider male paradigms of diaspora membership that emphasize affinity across not only time but also space. By examining the writings of Alice Walker, Michelle Cliff, and Ama Ata Aidoo, I explore how women write the diaspora as a collective that necessarily embraces our divergences and our intersections. Like these women, I struggle to navigate the social, cultural, and intellectual currents of diaspora membership. Just as the very notion of "diaspora" recognizes geographical dispersal, so too should our theories and practice recognize the consequent variations. With them, I call for a new progressivism that speaks of color, class, gender, and sexuality as integral to our sense of ourselves as a collective.

Along the way, I have been blessed with academic, social, and biological kin who have participated in ways immeasurable to the completion of this project. The research for this project was supported by grants from the Research Council and Kerr Libraries at Oregon State University, and the Council of Research and the College of Arts and Sciences at Louisiana State University. I would also like to thank the director and staff at The Moorland-Spingarn Research Center at Howard University. As well, I have benefited from a circle of scholars who encouraged, listened, read, and responded— none of these made easier by me.

To Heather Lee Miller and the staff at the Ohio State University Press, thanks for giving form to my vision. To my first academic family at Oregon State University, thank you. In my current academic home, Louisiana State University, I appreciate James Olney's generosity and careful reading and commentary on various versions of this book. I am especially indebted to the women from my writing group: Elsie Michie, Susannah Monta, and Katy

Powell, whose devoted energies and patience persisted through the metamorphoses. I must acknowledge my mentor family tree: Karla FC Holloway, Geneva Smitherman, Katherine Fishburn, Carol Mattingly, Robin Roberts, and Emily Toth—towering beacons whose scholarly strivings inspire me still. The best parts of this book bear the imprint of your influence.

I carry the mark of the endurance, faith, and love of my social matrix: Linda Strong-Leek, my sister in the struggle; Jennifer Cornell and Martin Hannigan, my partners in the valley, now across the sea; Roderick Hawkins, Marc Balthazar, and Randy Fontenot, my bayou family; your steadying presences are beyond measure and acclaim. For helping me to stay organized, I owe a special debt to Daina Mims. For reminding me to remain ever diligent and renewing my faith in *sisterhood,* I want to especially thank Ungelica Battiste, Clarisse Frazier, Micolette Thomas, and Tiffany Pitts. My academic pursuits have always been fostered by the love, faith, and support of my mentor and friend Gedney M. Howe III to whom I owe more than my language allows me to confess.

To my biological family, I owe the debt of myself. I hope I represent you well and bring fruits worthy of your toil. I dedicate this project to Mummy, my great-grandmother, whose guidance brought me to the places wherein I could do this work, and whose spirit sustains me even now. Finally, I thank His God for blessing me with all of these people, His gifts.

chapter one

How It Feels to Read Colored Me,[1] or "What is Africa to Me?"

This chapter's title, "How It Feels to Read Colored Me," indicates this book's goal: to contemplate a process of reading and writing the diaspora from one blackwoman diaspora studies scholar's point of view.[2] The project is complicated because the cultural identity of blackness has become contentious intellectual property. For the past decade, at least, the struggle has most conspicuously been waged by those who would name themselves "race men."[3] The term race *men* emphasizes how in this contest for intellectual property, we have experienced a privileging of a masculine theorizing that has all but erased the pragmatic aspects of black studies.[4] In fact, Hazel Carby directly takes on the intellectual tradition of African American race men in her eponymously titled critical study. Carby argues that W. E. B. Du Bois's intellectual project was not exclusively presenting a genealogy of race, the souls of the black nation. As well, Du Bois's raced nation was "determined by the nature of the struggle among black men over the bodies of women" (25). Black women scholars and writers have nonetheless continuously called for a (re)envisioning of practical theory in black studies, which to date has been so grounded in Du Bois's ideas. Indeed, Carby ends her analysis of Du Bois by asking, "To what extent do we still live with the politics of gender implicated in Du Bois' locating the black nation in a black male body?" (41). Just as Du Bois's influence has been noted in diaspora discourse, I translate Carby's inquiry to another constructed raced nation, the African diaspora. Like the Negro, diaspora people have been masculinized, and the diaspora has been claimed as an especially male place. Nonetheless, in a struggle focused on "saving their own [literary, scholarly, political, and social] lives," women critics, and women writers, too, have crafted an alternative theory of black folk (Christian, "Race for Theory" 358).[5]

The second half of the chapter title beckons us back to Countee Cullen's cogent example of the importance that Africa as location—in diaspora culture, but particularly in African American culture—has had and continues to have. In the first line of Cullen's "Heritage," the speaker asks, "What is Africa

1

to me?" The *me* is, most obviously, the black American, a Negro, revealing his "twoness." However, I contend that *me* could be any child of Africa's diaspora, exploring the foundation of an ethnicity defined by negotiating a relationship to an African past:

> *One three centuries removed*
> *From the scenes his father loved*
> *Spicy grove and banyan tree,*
> *What is Africa to me?* (italics in original; 250)

The speaker accepts that there is a connection between Africa and African America but ponders how that connection should be represented. Cullen crystallizes the ways in which our race men have theoretically contemplated diaspora kinship. The women writers I discuss inquire into the relationship between such textual and lived realities of diaspora membership, and they aim to negotiate kinship terms. The final words from Cullen's "Heritage" highlight one of the pragmatic obstacles:

> Lord forgive me if my need
> Sometimes shapes a human creed. (253)

These words make clear that because of the temporal distance emphasized earlier, the need to know and answer that yearning has facilitated the shaping of an Africa, a mythic grounding place.

This chapter situates Alice Walker, Michelle Cliff, and Ama Ata Aidoo on the continuum of writers who have endeavored to concretize the subjects created by W. E. B. Du Bois's theory of double consciousness. I engage a discourse of black cultural continuity and examine the fictions created within and written against this discourse. I expose contestations surrounding the idea that Blackness[6] signifies "all people of African descent—the Latin, the Jamaican, the Haitian, the Brazilian, the Caribbean, and the African American," because "although they were not born in Africa, they are still African people" (Kouyate B8). This cultural syncretism has led to the very development of the African diaspora—an ethnic collective defined as the population of indigenous Africans dispersed through systematic and/or planned movement from the African continent—and its intellectual and creative exploration as cultural text.

I explore the ways in which Walker, Cliff, and Aidoo use literature to examine how theoretical formulations of race become manifest in the lives of those who are conscripted by them. That is, these writers use their characters to create critical cultural fiction—works that explore culture itself. Though it could be argued that all literature explores some facet of culture, cultural fictions have positionality at their core. Going beyond mere explorations, these texts seek to first isolate and identify a particular cultural image, practice, or dilemma. Then, they use that cultural fact to query raced and cultural realities of their place.

In these diaspora places, the present is always linked to the past: race and slavery, Africa and her diaspora. For the African diaspora child, the present recalls the past in different ways. Killens, a black aesthetician, argued that a cultural matrix for Africans in the diaspora is necessary for their survival in the New World ("Brotherhood" 8). This "cultural reality" involves a synthesis of old and new into a new whole: a hybrid, Du Bois's notion of double consciousness. While Killens acknowledges the African influence on his sense of himself, others like Bruce Wright do not: "Black is where thatched temples burn / Incense to carved ebon-wood; / Where traders shaped my father's pain, / His person and his place, / Among dead statues in a frieze, / In the spectrum of his race" (145). Wright suggests, instead, a definitive difference between himself and his African ancestors. What is particularly powerful about Wright's rejection here is that he capsulizes the dilemma facing the descendants of Africans, both enslaved and free. First, Wright's African Americanness highlights black Americans' dominion over this area of intellectual inquiry, explaining Walker's continued journey into Africa in search of herself. As well, he indicates that "Black" lives in the land of "thatched temples," directing us to the issues of color that Michelle Cliff examines. Finally, his mention of "traders," and the homophonic and analogic relationship between *traders* in human cargo and the African *traitors* who sold their brothers, prepares us for Ama Ata Aidoo's explicit investigation of Africans' role in creating the diaspora. Wright emphasizes location in his comments. His focus is not only on the person of the diaspora child but also his "place."

This chapter introduces the ideas of race and place that permeate the concept of the diaspora as I examine it in this book. To do so, I begin with the men who have most influenced and, for the most part, shaped race(d) discourse. Then, I move to selected diaspora women's interpretations of that discourse. Although I call them diaspora women, I do so to suspend the singularity of African, Black, and Creole. I do not dispute that diaspora has monolithic potential. However, within my critical narrative, the diversities that diaspora signifies are allowed space to roam individually free. In fact, these differences simultaneously express historical and experiential intersections. The consciousness exposed in Aidoo's,

Walker's, and Cliff's writing demonstrates that the diaspora boundaries established by men like Nkrumah and Du Bois need not confine our politic, for just
as families expand with births, kinship systems can be fluid, terms renegotiated,
and boundaries redefined.

The Legacy of "Race": Membership in a Race Family

The legacy of "race" and the kinship it signifies were bequeathed to writers
of African descent living in the United States as early as 1837. In "An Address
to the Colored People of the United States," Frederick Douglass (re)estab-
lished the common bond amongst all people of the same color.[7] The means
through which this sense of cohesion among blacks was achieved in the
United States took many forms, ranging from arguments about common
ancestry and shared color to the development of a notion of an ethnic community. This range is represented in the switch from a belief that blackness
denotes only a biological group to one in which blackness names a sociohistorical collective (Appiah 41; Marable 295–96).

Like the transition from biological race to sociopolitical ethnicity, the
processes—cultural and social—by which Africans became African Americans
were phasic. Phase one was assimilation toward the direction of Europeans and
an adoption of the white negative attitude toward all things African. Next
came the secular/evangelical phase wherein secular wars and evangelical missions accelerated assimilation. Along with the Christianization of the evangelical missions came access to literacy.[8] Literacy marked the crafting of the black
subject, its location in a specific place, and an excavation of its African linkages. Hence, we can say that written blackness represents not only identity but
also positionality. To be black is to claim for oneself a particular sociocultural
history and position oneself within a sociopolitical narrative.

In 1897 W. E. B. Du Bois submitted that "the history of the world is the
history, not of individuals, but of groups, not of nations, but of races"
("Conservation" 21). He further added that anyone "who ignores or seeks to
override the race idea in human history ignores and overrides the central
thought of all human history" (21). Holding to his ideas about race, Du Bois
argued prophetically that the difficulty of the twentieth century would be
"the problem of the color line" (*Souls* 13). For Du Bois, race "is a vast family
of human beings" defined, in part, by "purely physical characteristics"
("Conservation" 21, 20). Du Bois articulates this principle in his definition
of the Negro as part of the American geographical family, but also as part of
the African race family, the conflation of two seemingly disparate ethnic enti-

ties. Michelle Cliff, in fact, makes this connection between color and race particularly problematic, and in that way challenges the sanctity with which Du Bois's notion of the color line has been held.

The 1990s saw the theoretical and pragmatic concept of race itself become the focus of debate. The constructs of race-as-family and race-as-nation imply not only a biological and sociological explanation for racial divisions, but also a cultural and historical one. Ama Ata Aidoo explores this history and undertakes an inquiry into how that history manifests itself in relationships between continental Africans and their diaspora kin. Though Aidoo is unique in many ways for her vigilance in exploring this subject, she revisits a conversation that took place between Nigerian Thomas Echewa and black American novelist John A. Williams, and the response by John Oliver Killens.

In its January 1965 issue, *Negro Digest* published Thomas Echewa's "Africans vs Afro-Americans," wherein the then-student of journalism at Columbia University addressed the relationship between Africans and black Americans. Echewa's discussion catalyzed a heated exchange that offers insight into the cultural and political basis of the issues we are dealing with here. Significant to a cultural critic's perspective, he tells us that attempts to understand the relationship between people of African descent throughout the world often eschew the basic reality that "when a Negro American asks an African if they are the same and the African says 'No,' he means only that he is an African and the Negro is an American" (34).

Echewa highlights centuries of black/African experience in America, manifested in an alternative cultural canon—the ideology and practices of "one three centuries removed" (Cullen 250). He especially notes the effects of geographical distance in his assertion that it is "too much to expect that because Negroes and Africans have a common *distant* ancestry, every African and every Negro American should get along" (34–35; emphasis mine).

Echewa's remarks did not go unanswered, and in the September 1965 issue John A. Williams, in his "Open Letter to an African" entitled "The Way It Is," asserted that Africans see black Americans through Europeans' eyes, eyes that have obscured their seeing "[black Americans'] total participation" in America (29). Williams focused on the word *Negro* and what it identifies for Africans about African Americans, that for the African, the Negro represents "a man without a tribe," and such a man is "next to worthless" in a society—Africa—where membership in a clan is identity. In Aidoo's *Dilemma* Eulalie discovers the power of this social distance.

Aidoo's inquiries are shaped by her experiences as a Ghanaian, and the political and intellectual bonds between her country and mine are legion.

These bonds were forged by a kinship between Nkrumah, Ghana's first president, and the United States's premiere black intellectual, Du Bois, who saw themselves as Pan African brothers. DuBois and Nkrumah bridged the distance of time and space, forging an intellectual, political, and social brotherhood that suspended the specific histories of each in his own place. This exchange illustrates that for both Echewa and Williams, the issue is a matter of both diaspora politics and sociocultural pride. Each defends his right to pledge allegiance to the geographical and cultural spaces of their birth, to their particular cultural identities, even at the expense of their ethnic bond to each other. Michelle Cliff would add, however, that it is this notion of a preexistent, constant bond of heritage that complicates relations. Such presumption erases the particularity of the individual and replaces her with an imagined person. As well, Walker and Aidoo would join Cliff in arguing that Williams's terming of this club a "brotherhood" equally dissipates the gender dynamic within the historical drama of African diaspora relations.

A decade after the exchange between Echewa and Williams, Aidoo wrote her *Dilemma,* which exposes the pragmatic difficulties of adhering to the race-as-family model to the exclusion of geographic and historical particularity.[9] The women that I gather here offer another alternative that is not necessarily a middle ground, but a space wherein the relationship between Africa and her diaspora children is always being negotiated and is never fixed. They embrace the notion of themselves as relative strangers and see this distant closeness not as a basis for acrimonious debate but for constructive conversations about kinship, consciousness, and positionality. Walker, Cliff, and Aidoo are fiction writers and cultural critics who recognize that they are at once present in the space that they are attempting to define—Africa—and simultaneously absent or excluded from that space. They refute historical suggestions that in order to bridge the gulf of being absent and present, one need only demonstrate that the African self somehow latently resides in the diaspora self. Instead, these women inquire into how the notion of a diaspora self articulates itself in their geographical spaces. Place is an especially telling lens for reading their diaspora inquiries. In past discussions the United States and Africa have dominated and silenced Caribbeans, and the Creole is erased from the race family, making Michelle Cliff's voice even more necessary and pronounced.

Cliff contests Du Bois's suggestion that race is culture and culture is race, and she reveals the degree to which when we speak about "race" we are actually speaking locally, though intimating diaspora relevance. While she does not champion a postmodernist erasure of race, her fiction underscores the relevance of *ethnicity,* referring to groups of people who may or may not share a geographical space but share common ancestry and cultural patterns of behavior. Even though racial biology is refutable, we cannot dismiss ethnicity as a valid construct or reject a focus on common descent.[10] Furthermore, we must honestly discuss ethnicity and its connections to discussions of race, as well as examine the effects of racialized ideology on those who are its subjects. It is my project here to focus most particularly on how ethnic identity is represented in literature by three female members of Du Bois's raced family. Each has inherited a historical understanding of herself that is as much tied to place as it is to ideologies of what colored and raced bodies mean. Walker, Cliff, and Aidoo each build upon their diaspora inheritance.

As Barbara J. Fields makes clear, race is "an ideological construct *and* an historical product" ("Ideology and Race" 149; emphasis mine). Moreover, Fields contends that an ideology consists in "the descriptive vocabulary of day to day existence, through which people make sense of the social reality that they live and create from day to day" ("Slavery" 109). Race, then, continues to exist, not because we inherited it, but because we recreate it every day. I would argue that one way in which we remake it is through discourse. Fields's discussion of "race" highlights the nature of its tropological functioning. A trope, existing adjacent to literal or conventional language, (re)creates meaning and (re)establishes realms of signification. Simultaneously, it is a movement *from* and a movement *towards.* For example, in Cliff's *No Telephone to Heaven* and *Abeng,* Clare Savage represents the trope "creole," as the Creole is a racial merger of the savage and the civilized; the racialized subject seeks clarity of position vis-à-vis her duality. Her signifying name emphasizes the ways in which our readings of her character are shaped by the way racial reasoning translates her name for us.[11]

Instead of confining us to and constricting us by theoretical wranglings, the writings I gather in this book examine "the lived experiences of those within racial groups" (Outlaw 77). They move from discourse on *what* race is to conversations about *how* race and experiences of it are place specific. For example, "race" as an interpretive lens focalizes Aidoo's fiction. She creates a world where black and white peoples use their understanding of race to interpret and (re)create Ghana and Ghanaians. Because both these raced peoples are located in the West, their readings intersect in interesting ways. Aidoo, Walker, and Cliff design the diaspora as an ethnic collective, yet they expose site-specific understandings and interpretations of life within that collective.

Writer, Reader, and Critic: A Part and Place for Each One

As we attempt to explore how race functions in the act of production of African diaspora texts, we should recall Uzo Esonwanne's suggestion that to talk of "race" is to speak of "private investments" as well as "past and ongoing grievances" (565). The notion of private investments is key to understanding why it was and is so important, first of all, to essentialize race—as Du Bois did and as Fields does. Though Esonwanne does not define "private invest- ments," I conclude that he means these are the estimates of what is to be gained through endorsing a particular definition of race. Esonwanne posi- tions "race" within Dilthey's concept of "the hermeneutic circle."[12] The hermeneutic circle is a reference to the complex process of understanding whereby the parts of anything cannot be understood without some sense of the whole to which they belong. Conversely, we cannot comprehend the whole to which things belong without first grasping the parts that form it.

In essence, we are constantly obliged to move back and forth between the whole and its parts in our attempts to arrive at an understanding. With respect to "race," we must explore what is invested in furthering beliefs con- cerning "race" if we are to understand how it relates to interpretation. The private investments are some of the parts that constitute "race" as a whole. "Race" functions to order the reality of those who live within its confines (i.e., blacks and other consciously aware racial groups), and as such it affords meaning to certain aspects of their experience.[13] Ironically, to argue his case Esonwanne offers a critique of Henry Louis Gates's *The Signifying Monkey.* Briefly, in arguing that the trip through the Middle Passage did not erase all traces of Africanisms, Gates compares Yoruba Èsù Elegbarà to the African American signifying monkey. In this comparison, Esonwanne argues, Gates elides significant differences between the two figures of his comparison. Gates's attempt to connect these two figures is only successful if we *re*define Èsù Elegbarà outside of Yoruba culture. This book avoids this pitfall by con- sidering each writer in her cultural and national contexts, and by examining the ways in which that particularity articulates their similar diaspora con- sciousnesses and their sometimes conflicting positions in the diaspora kin- ship system.

Diaspora Consciousness: Ghanaian and Jamaican Intersections

In constructing my idea of a diaspora consciousness, I draw on VèVè Clark's argument that the New Negro, Indigenist, and Negritude movements in the

1920s and 1930s in the United States, the Caribbean, and Africa, respectively, "invented a construct, the African diaspora, referring to the phenomenon and history of African American [*sic*] displacement in the New World" (41). Clark outlines what she terms diaspora literacy, referring to readers' knowledge of African, African American, and Caribbean literatures, and this literacy includes a comprehension of the texts from an "informed, indigenous perspective," a perspective engendered by awareness of the "historical, social, cultural and political development generated by lived and textual experiences" (42). She identifies several discursive strategies; it is her third, "reformation of form," that most informs my discussion of Walker, Cliff, and Aidoo. This principle is a "reduplicative posture which assumes and revises Du Bois' double consciousness" (42). This deliberate process of revision is directed toward not simply exploring the diaspora, but toward creating a space for negotiation of the historical, social, cultural, and political consequences of diaspora membership. While Du Bois's double consciousness speaks to African American conditions, Cliff and Aidoo infuse the concept with emphases specific to Jamaican Creole and Ghanaian realities.

Thus, an engaged identity consciousness is constructed, one that revolves around a diaspora politic. This section outlines how as revisions of Du Boisian "double consciousness," Nkrumahan Pan Africanism and Garveyan political theory facilitate the construction of African American, Ghanaian, and Jamaican diaspora-conscious voices. These three men have the same ideological impulses, in three different places, and the practical manifestations of their beliefs are defined by the conditions of their home. Moving beyond masculinized concerns, Walker, Aidoo, and Cliff commit to not only Clark's notion of diaspora literacy, but also to a diaspora politic.

Ghana, one of the first African nations to gain independence from colonialism, was also the home of Kwame Nkrumah, its first national president. Nkrumah made African involvement in a diaspora politic a theoretical reality. Setting aside other political debates surrounding Nkrumah's leadership, he is noted for his treatises on and commitment to Pan Africanism.[14] What is most interesting in this context, though, is how Nkrumah expressed his Pan Africanist vision, his firm belief that "the independence of Ghana [was] meaningless unless it [was] linked with the total liberation of the African continent" (*Spectre* 10). Nkrumah clearly identifies that his ideas about Pan Africanism were guided and informed by the "work of the early pioneers of Pan Africanism such as H. Sylvester William, Dr. W. E. B. Du Bois, Marcus Garvey, and George Padmore, none of whom were born in Africa [but their work has] become a treasured part of Africa's history" (*Spectre* 5).

Nkrumah forged a platform that aligned historical, intellectual, and political struggles. He notes that part of moving Africa toward a productive and independent future requires a "recovery and reawakening" of its past. The concern for continental Africans is reclaiming their historical and cultural space, a "regeneration of Africa" ("Glorious Past" 11). Although Africans are not a "homogeneous race, [they] possess a common fundamental sentiment which is everywhere manifest, crystallizing itself into one common controlling idea" ("Glorious Past" 10): Pan Africanism, "the spectre of black power."[15] Though Nkrumah counseled with black American intellectuals, his primary focus for Pan Africanism was continental, with ramifications and implications for the diaspora. Nonetheless, it seems fair to suggest that his dilemma was how to unite and liberate Africa, a vast project indeed, while simultaneously directing that unified attention to related liberatory struggles of blacks elsewhere. Aidoo's *Our Sister Killjoy* embarks on this project. The protagonist Sissie struggles to remain faithful to Nkrumah's theory. Yet the novel simultaneously articulates a position that contests Nkrumah's, offering that there is no *one* controlling idea.

Providing an intersection between Du Bois and Nkrumah, Jamaica-born Marcus Garvey ventured to take the shared history and the theoretical model of Pan Africanism to create a practical plan for improving the conditions of black life. Garvey is perhaps most noted for his battle cry "Africa for the Africans, those at home and those abroad," but he played a significant role in the relationship between West Indian and U.S. blacks. Garvey saw their plights as one and the same, and organized the Black Star Line, a steamship company that shipped African produce to the Americas and the Caribbean. Since emancipation in 1838, Jamaica, Cliff's literary home, has been held as an archetypal society that has fostered a public model of progress in the achievement of egalitarian ideals and interracial harmony. Marcus Garvey, for example, in a 1914 piece submitted to *The Tourist* (London) and later printed in Jamaica's *Gleaner,* wrote of Jamaica as the "pearl of the Antilles," and described the African presence thus:

> It is just seventy six years since the Jamaican negro emerged from his shackles, and within this period of time, he has accomplished wonders. . . . In Jamaica the descendants of old slaves are to be found in all departments of social, intellectual, administrative, commercial and industrial activity. . . . There is no friction of colour, and the day is yet to come for anyone to hear anything disparaging said about the difference of race among the people. Unlike the American negro the Jamaican lives in an atmosphere of equality and comradeship, hence the outrages

that are characteristic of America are quite unheard of in the island. (Garvey 42–43)

However, responses to the printing of Garvey's ideas reveal a counter-version that has occupied a continual place in the minds of Jamaicans and that has repeatedly been invoked in the numerous popular movements of self-liberation and expression. In his letter to the editor, Charles S. Shirley of Lawrence Tavern asks:

> [W]hat is anyone's idea of prosperity who thinks that the black man of Jamaica is prospering fairly well? . . . No fairminded man who knows the actual condition of the black man in Jamaica—and the brown or colored people too as far as that's concerned—can conscientiously say that the black man's lot in Jamaica is anything desirable. There is actually no comparison between the condition of the black[s] in Jamaica and [their] brother[s] in America. (qtd. in Garvey 47)

The latter conception of Jamaica is at considerable variance with that of the racial paradise. Furthermore, it directly contradicts Garvey's biblicized idea of the island as a Babylon for blacks.

Unlike Nkrumah's Ghana and Ghanaians, the peoples of the Caribbean, and of Jamaica particularly, are the products of the most sustained and intense European colonial domination experienced by any present-day population, and for some, the process has not yet ended. Because the British Colonial Office administered the islands separately, allowing the plantocracies on the individual islands to engage in economic competition with each other, Caribbean societies have always been politically and economically fragmented. Most relevant to my inquiry of Cliff, island societies, with their social, cultural, and structured pluralism, are divided along the lines of slave and free, of white, colored, and black, making the region an internally divided body with culturally dissimilar extremities. Despite the theoretical influence of Du Bois and Nkrumah, and even Garvey, one can scarcely defend the notion of an integrated Caribbean, or justify speaking of the Caribbean, or the West Indies, as a holistic entity.

Though Du Bois and Garvey were Pan Africanists, desiring freedom for the world's population of African peoples, their approaches were quite different. Du Bois built a black intellectual movement, while Garvey managed to organize a black mass movement. Cliff's Clare Savage demonstrates how the Caribbeans syncretize these influences, for she is an intellectual and a radical revolutionary. Where Du Bois and Nkrumah talked about the history and culture of the African race family, Garvey endeavored to unite that family through a consolidated approach to their social, cultural, political, and economic circumstances. Garvey, with Nkrumah and Du Bois, established the traditions into which Cliff, Aidoo, and Walker were born, the legacy of kinship they each inherited. Likewise, I read their fiction as engaging their inheritance, but, more importantly, also fashioning the legacy they themselves will leave.

Ideological presuppositions come from traditions. I reference Gadamer's notion of tradition, which suggests that we can consciously know our own tradition, and know it in such a way that when we encounter another's tradition we can distinguish the two and reach the pinnacle of understanding that he calls the "fusion of horizons" (306–7). He acknowledges that no reader comes to a text without prejudices and presumptions. However, we must distinguish enabling prejudices from hindering ones; this distinction is crucial to self-understanding as well as to understanding Others (295–96). In order to conceptualize this distinguishing process, we must foreground "temporal distance and its significance for understanding" (296). Walker, Cliff, and Aidoo not only evince some understanding of temporal distance, but they also struggle to negotiate the importance of this concept for diaspora consciousness and a kinship grounded in acceptance of our same difference.

Examining the Culture of Fiction, or the Fictions on/of Culture

In many ways, this is a project of and about cross-cultural readings, readings that insert "a ceaseless dialogue between hardened conventions and eclipsed and half eclipsed otherness within an intuitive self that moves endlessly into flexible patterns, arcs, or bridges of community" (W. Harris 1983, xviii). Literary texts provide a forum wherein the African diaspora child's dialogue between her "eclipsed and half eclipsed otherness" takes place. As we have seen, this dialogue with the African past has been quite ceaseless and involves building a bridge between the past and present. Though the dialogue has been entered from various vantage points, the ambition in each case has been to announce that while African American and Jamaican social systems have responded to the conditions of life in the United States and Jamaica, many contemporary forms of their culture establish and/or represent direct continuities from Africa. And Ghana has, historically, been the Mecca to which black diasporans travel to (re)discover the bonds that these continuities suggest.

Though African Americans and Jamaicans are not African, by quoting Eddy Harris I suggest that they are more than "hybrid." Harris's position echoes a belief that being of "mixed breed" is disturbing because it implies "not whole." However, this nonwholeness is especially useful from a critical perspective. As Bakhtin tells us, hybridization, "the mixture of two social languages within the limits of a single utterance," is one of the three basic linguistic "devices" employed in the novel (358). The device is even more appropriately framed within the diaspora context. To clarify my point, let us examine the term *African American*. Itself a hybrid construction, it contains at least two social voices, "two utterances, two . . . semantic . . . belief systems" (Bakhtin 304). Meant to designate a single population, black people in the United States, it also implicates another population, Africans from the continent. The latter has been subsumed beneath the former, or the former has been inscribed upon the latter.

Similarly, we can examine the term *creole*. *Creole* is replete with contradictions and intersections; Judith Raiskin rightly claims that the term is "elastic" (3). Edward K. Brathwaite suggests that the term is derived "from a combination of two Spanish words *criar* (to create, to imagine, to establish, to found, to settle) and *colon* (a colonist, a founder, a settler) into *criollo:* a committed settler, one identified with the area of settlement, one native to the settlement though not ancestrally indigenous to it" (10). However, the *Oxford English Dictionary* records the word as originating from *criollo* and in addition to referring to "unsullied" whiteness, it can refer to "persons of mixed racial ancestry" resulting from colonialism. The term also references linguistic and cultural syncretism. Like its sister reference *African American, creole* manifests the intersections between a past racial purity, a present of colonial intermixing, and a future of doubly identified peoples.[16]

Either way, the African American and Jamaican Creole speak with two cultural voices, and they are named to reflect this "twoness." It is this hybridization that complicates the cross-cultural reading endeavor, and necessitates the parallel inclusion of one African woman's voice, informing the hybridity of both the African American and the Creole, and responding to her implication in their identity fashioning. Bakhtin's notion of heteroglossic utterance captures the essence of this project, to allow the different diaspora sites to usher forth, through literary work, their voices, and to position these voices in conversation with, sometimes even across, each other. They speak across each other because these discursive modes are determined by a set of linguistic protocols whose range and governance far exceed our conscious control. This revises Gadamer, and nicely so.

Nonetheless, Gadamer offers an ideal, in my view, toward which we should strive. An utterance, a text, is a border phenomenon; it takes place between speakers—readers and writers—and is embedded in social factors. It exists on the border of the tradition(s) that produce it and the larger tradition(s) within which its producer and consumer exist. Hence, we must explore not only the large body of the texts, but the grammars of discourse that delimit and constitute cultural experience: the sites of our cultural memory, the sources of cultural fiction.

Cultural fictions are created because of certain predispositions toward Africa(n texts) that operate unchallenged. I do not suggest that it is possible to read without prejudice. Since we always understand from within our own horizons, there can be no nonpositional understanding of anything, because understanding involves lived experiences. We always understand by reference to our own experience. However, as critics and readers, we must question when/if our version of cultural reality is being placed over and above the experience of cultural reality encountered in the text. In other words, hermeneutic understanding requires the acknowledgment of the *two* traditions, *two* experiences confronting each other in the interpretive act, and requires the diasporic separation of roots and routes (Gilroy 1992).

Negotiating the Borders of Diaspora Identity

An outsider can never see what the natives see, only what they see with. In attempting to grasp the customs the Other uses to see, we must seek out the "symbolic forms . . . in terms of which . . . people actually represent themselves to one another" (Geertz 228). We must attempt not to enter their horizon—in Heinz-Georg Gadamer's sense of the word—but to grasp how they have constructed it and maintain themselves within it. In terms of reading cross-culturally and interpreting cultural fiction, the critic must attempt to ascertain what symbols and discourses the text uses to construct the tradition within which the text exists. While Clifford Geertz would call this an attempt to secure "the native's point of view," I explain it via the concept "com ya cyant know more than been ya." Simply translated, this proverb from the Gullah tradition explains that newcomers to a place cannot understand it better than one who has been around for quite some time. It is a warning against presumption and an invitation to dialogue. It is with this spirit that I use it to title chapter 2 of this project.

Chapter 2 presents Alice Walker's *Possessing* as a sankofa narrative, wherein she unearths her ancestral past in order to construct her womanist-informed future. An African American woman, Walker is heavily influenced by the discourses on race, blackness, and critical revisions that I highlighted in the first two sections of this chapter. Of all the writers engaged in this project, Walker is the most celebrated and the best known, and her popularity and widespread acclaim and criticism make her a viable portal for entry into conversations on kinship and politic. Walker travels back to Africa through the physical, psychic, and historical memories of her foremothers. She attempts to read the signs of their stories for an understanding of that past. Specifically, I follow a trajectory from Meridian to Tashi, arguing that all of Walker's women, like herself, are searching for their kin, looking for the social, cultural, and political space into which they can insert themselves. Reading her writings collectively, as part of her own ongoing autobiographical narrative, makes clear the legacy of race that informs much blackwomen's literature. Indeed, Walker's theoretical, pragmatic, and political womanism is an apt point of departure for developing and understanding sistered kinship.

Walker's trek to Africa, a space she has crafted in and as fiction, negotiates past impulses to either present Africa as Edenic or barbaric. Issues of fictional representation and the effects of such on politics explains my titling chapter 3 "Dis here is fe me territory": White Sand, Blue Water, and Cliff's Space for the Creole." Chapter 3 explores Michelle Cliff's ancestral and historical topography, which compels her to (re)configure a local narrative of origin, to retake her home territory. These narratives are situated in Jamaica but reach out in one direction to the United States and in the other to Ghana; within this study, Cliff's writings form a "bridge." The term *bridge* is a chronotope, temporal and spatial, providing "an optic for reading texts as x-rays of the forces at work in the cultural system from which they spring" (Bakhtin 425).[17] Cliff's narratives connect African and African American voices on the subjects of geography and identity, and they show how notions of blackness complicate both. Cliff's writings manifest a step in the progression of diaspora women's political and personal agency. We move from the victimization of these women by patriarchal forces—evidenced by Tashi in Walker's *Possessing*—to Clare Savage, a woman who confronts the forces that constrict her full experience of herself. Although Clare dies, she exhibits a critical approach to her life choices as prescribed by a history of person and place. Clare, unlike the romanticized, empathetic Tashi, is not easily embraced, yet the reader is still made to feel the righteousness of her rage. These two characters manifest the push-pull of the diaspora relationship. How to both recognize Africa as historical homeland and accept the barbaric circumstances that compelled that separation is precisely the concern that drives Aidoo's writing.

I title chapter 4 "Blackwomen Always Seem to Be Going Through *Changes*" to reference Aidoo's novel, but also to capture the struggles of the diaspora daughter. Clare's rage and alienation and Tashi's psychic instability are fostered by misunderstanding(s) and misrepresentations of diaspora history and black people's affinity and difference. Aidoo explores the event that casts the worlds inhabited by Walker and Cliff—the history of African dispersal—and she shatters representations of the protective African kin, exploited by the deceptive tactics of Europeans. All of her works allude to the diasporic relationship. Particularly she asks how such relations would change if all members talked openly about the circumstances of that historical event: the catalysts for dispersal; the psychological, physical, spiritual, and emotional results of the dispersal; and reconciliation after centuries of very different yet connected realities. In this chapter, I use Ama Ata Aidoo's writing to examine the ur-sister in the diaspora sistered kinship relationship.

As I previously noted, there is a peculiar political relationship between Aidoo's Ghana and Walker's United States.[18] As a former British territory, Ghana is also linked colonially to Cliff's Jamaica. The connection between the characters that Aidoo constructs and those of Walker and Cliff resides in their desire to know themselves through a knowledge of their sisters and the history that grounds their kinship. In the main, the relationship between Africans and African Americans has been a theme in African American literature for centuries. While a connection to the past has been a recurrent theme for both black American male and female writers, African writers have not shown as much concentrated interest in exploring this historical connection.[19] In the canon of female literature, though, Ama Ata Aidoo is a notable exception; her writings reflect a commitment to diaspora consciousness.

Read alongside Alice Walker's construction of an African woman and Cliff's struggle to claim her Creoleness, Aidoo's gendered identity narratives signal a closeness among these three women and their characters, one that should neither be taken for granted nor overlooked.[20] As Aidoo herself explains, being Ghanaian has encouraged her desire to heal the fracture enacted by the dismemberment of the continent and the African family:

> Maybe it is because I come from a people for whom, for some reason, the connection with African-America or the Caribbean was a living thing, something of which we were always aware. In Nkrumah's Ghana one met African-Americans and people from the Caribbean. . . . I think the whole question of how it was that so many of our people could be enslaved and sold is very important. . . . It is an area that must be probed. It probably holds one of the keys to our future. (qtd. in James 20–21)

Aidoo links not only a critical assessment of diaspora relations as key to the success of the continent's future, but also the role of women in the creation of this future.[21] This dual concern about the role of women and the articulation of diaspora history conflates to found the conscious politic of sistered kinship that I see manifest in Aidoo's writing, and Walker's and Cliff's, as well.

The literary analyses in chapters 2, 3, and 4, though, center primarily on the diaspora consciousness aspect of this book's focus, and posit that this consciousness grounds their sistered kinship. However, the idea of a sistered kinship recognizes the sex/gender divide as well as the idea of race as family that diaspora connotes. Focusing, then, on the sexed voice in these writers, chapter 5 is appropriately titled "'Write it in. . . . Put the sex right up on in there!': Walker, Cliff, and Aidoo Sexualize and (Re)map the Diaspora." Concluding my conversation with the sisters, I engage their specific speaking to issues of female sexuality, specifically homosexuality, as an essential consideration of sistered kinship. My notions of kinship recall not only Pan Africanist thinkers, but also Claude Lévi-Strauss's theory of kinship systems and women's roles within them. Women are primarily *objects* of exchange, and he describes the exchange of women as a necessary element in "the system of binding men together" (Lévi-Strauss 481).[22] Within such a kinship system, sexual behavior is heterosexual and compulsorily so. As well, this *man*date reinforces the centrality of men within women's subjective being, in fact making them objects.

While the notion of a social contract between men infers a certain male homosociality, an economy of male sameness founded on their equal participation in the economy of woman exchange, no similar relationship between women can exist. As such, homophobia develops as a means to suppress women's ability to share in men's economy of power and clearly establish the prominence of maleness as a measure of that economy. The idea here is that men use homophobia to assert their own untainted maleness while simultaneously banning women from developing homosocial systems, which, when formed, are as equally empowering for women as they are for men.[23]

The notion of women's role as a binding of men intersects with the politics of black nationalism, which are in many ways mirrored in diaspora studies. Within black politics, male homosociality is maintained through the concepts of "race as family" and "race as nation" that I discussed earlier. Particularly, though, the family and nation depend on (1) woman as mother, reproducing the family and hence building the nation, and thus (2) heterosexuality.[24]

I want to be careful here to emphasize that I am neither outwardly accepting nor rejecting analyses that equate the suppression of homosexual subjectivity and of "raced" subjectivity. Yet, as part of their renegotiation of the notion of the race family, Walker, Cliff, and Aidoo necessarily delegitimize narratives that present blackwomen's sexuality as inextricable from a relationship to/with (black) men.[25]

Sexuality in the writings of Aidoo, Cliff, and Walker parallels narratives of the body geography. When Walker's Tashi journeys back to Olinka, M'Lissa inquires as to what an American looks like. In response, Tashi tells her "an American looks like me" (*Possessing* 210). Eulalie, too, is an American, and she tells Ato, when he challenges her over the language she uses to refer to his family, "I speak the way I was born to speak, like an American" (*Dilemma* 87). Both of these women acknowledge that the African who comes to America and resides in the United States of America—either in 1819, 1965, or 2000, either through slavery or immigration—eventually becomes American. Though these bodies carry traces of Africa, inscriptions of Africa, they are American bodies. Likewise, when Kitty Savage travels to America, she cannot recognize a kinship in her coworkers, because the color(ed) chasm that separates them from her—as well as her from them—seems unbridgeable. This is the reality that people of the black Atlantic must face, a relative strangeness.

Indeed, my analyses here are informed by the recognition that any diaspora consciousness is founded upon a fiction of place. For me, then, diaspora consciousness neither idolizes nor disregards Africa. The relationship to Africa grounds its politic, but the conscience of the sisters acknowledges that Africa is the text that must be simultaneously read and (re)constructed. Through these dialogic operations, Walker, Cliff, Aidoo, and I read the possibilities for sistered kinship and negotiate the political, social, economic, and pragmatic politic of any diasporic consciousness.

chapter two

"Com ya cyant 'no mo than been ya": Walker's Sankofa Narrative(s)

In his 1991 film *Sankofa,* Haile Gerima represents one African American woman's experience with and in Africa. The title of the film, Gerima declares, is taken from Akan and means "looking back to go forward." The film underscores the recovery of the ancestor/ancestral past "as an enabling metaphor," a "revisioning of cultural mythologies" (Holloway 2). The particular cultural mythologies central to *Sankofa* and to my study of Alice Walker focus on the relationship between African and African American women and the importance of ancestral experiences as a means of informing our own. Walker searches her ancestral mothers' gardens, and in the search finds Zora Neale Hurston, whose work in anthropology and folklore informs Walker's craft. As *Sankofa* situates an African American woman into the center of diaspora history, so Hurston provides Walker with a model for excavating that history and anthropologizing it as folkloric text. As the film narrates Mona/Shola's realization that her past must be claimed and understood, Alice Walker's fictions narrate her desire, as a descendant of "stolen Africans, to step out of the ocean/from the wounds of the ships and claim her story" (Gerima 81).[1]

The notion of "sankofa" provides a frame for analyzing Alice Walker's *Possessing the Secret of Joy.* The sankofa proverb warns one to know the past, so the other part of this chapter title contains a warning: one must always look to the ancestors, to those who came before, for guidance and information. Walker attempts to abide by these dicta in her construction of Tashi's narrative.[2] Using the film as a point of departure, this chapter reads Walker's fiction as her sankofa journey and as manifestations of her story as a diaspora sister.

The opening scenes of the film introduce us to the protagonist Mona, an African American female fashion model, scantily clad and wearing makeup that figures her as savage and exotic. She is being photographed by a white male photographer, and we only see his hands and hear him direct her: "Mona, more sex." This scene's sexual overtones continue as Mona writhes around on the ground and the photographer hovers over her, grunting encouragingly. This figurative rape recalls the intersection between economic and sexual exploitation of black women during slavery. A tribesman admonishes the visitors that they are trespassing on sacred ground, and their presence and behavior is a desecration. He advances toward Mona and shouts "'sankofa,' you must know your past" in his native tongue. Frightened, Mona runs to the white photographer who positions himself between her and the perceivably angry and hostile tribesman. This positioning symbolizes European distortion of diaspora history, separating blackwomen from their kin. The tribesman's warning is prophetic; Mona follows the tour group into the dungeons and discovers that she has literally been transported into a life of slavery. She and the others are carried to a slave ship and brought to America, where she becomes a house slave regularly raped by her master. Shola becomes Mona's ancestral figure, one whose remembering frames Mona's present experiences.

The ancestral relationship is further emphasized in the film through the intersecting narratives of Mona/Shola and Nunu. Born in Africa and manifesting a commitment to maintain her relationship with her native land through rituals, Nunu represents Mona's/Shola's biological as well as spiritual mother. When we first meet her, her gaze arrests the viewer; it is a tool she later uses to disarm her white master, which results in his death. She speaks very little; her influence and reverence are all located in her ability to look commandingly. Her maternal gaze encapsulates her creative, instructive, and destructive power. While the film criticizes Mona, taking her back to slavery to relive those atrocities so as to arrive at a fuller understanding of her place, Nunu is honored for her fearless response to slavery; she is a slave in flesh only. She refuses to be affected by the white gaze; instead, she manifests what bell hooks calls the "oppositional gaze," whereby her gaze changes and creates a reality in which she has subjective power ("Oppositional Gaze").

Sankofa operates within Karla Holloway's ideas of an enabling narrative. Mona's/Shola's cultural myth narrative is infused with Nunu's ancestral presence, allowing for Shola's (re)birth and (re)fashioning. Nunu, as the embodiment of African ritual and practice, a tenacious resistance, and an unyielding spirit, enables Shola. In the end, Mona's becoming an ancestor leads her to abandon modeling, a significant life change. The film invites us to know that her decision comes as a result of her newfound awareness of the past, a past she now carries with her into the future. In fact, at the film's end Mona turns to see Nunu smiling; they are reconnected on the shores of West Africa, positioning themselves as significant parts of each other's cultural narrative.

Like Mona, Walker explains that when she entered the House of Slaves on Gorée Island for the purpose of filming, the place brought a deep "feeling of sorrow" over her as she considered her "maternal ancestors" who were held there (*Warrior Marks* 74). Touching the chains and being then able to hear and see the people once bound by them, Walker explains that "the thought of [our maternal ancestors] crossing the ocean in the holds of ships in chains, with their vulvas stitched almost completely shut, nearly drove me round the bend" (74). Though she can imagine the pain these women felt, to truly know it she must (re)call one of them, and Tashi is her conjuring of such an ancestral figure. Like Gerima's film, the fiction of *Possessing* contains a diasporic cultural evaluation. The novel is a journey into the life and world of Tashi, an Olinkan woman who has recently emigrated to the United States. The narrative details the emotional, psychological, spiritual, and sexual trauma she experiences as a result of her compliance with traditions that sanction ritual female circumcision.[3] The primary focus of my analysis, however, is not ritual female circumcision, but Walker's narrating of her connection to Africa.

As Gina Dent tells us in "Black Pleasure, Black Joy," *Possessing* "forces us to confront *not* the history of female circumcision, but the mythical use of this particularity as a point of entry into the analysis of [black people's] ever elusive connections to Africa" (3). Instead, this ritual of/for/on the body becomes a central vehicle for crafting Walker's female characters—Tashi and M'Lissa. These two women emblematize Walker's sankofa journey. We begin the novel trying to understand Tashi, an African American, but we can only do so once we have been introduced to her African foremother M'Lissa. Their relationship bears out the sankofa proverb's truth.

This is made obvious in the text's final scene. Women gathered to witness Tashi's execution have been "warned they must not sing"; instead, these women allow their bare-bottomed female babies to be their voices. Representing the future, the little women are lifted onto their mothers' shoulders; the sounds of the babies' voices represent the women's collective protest against a male authority—embodied by the armed male guards. The presence of these voiced, gendered bodies challenges the authority that would silence them and dictate their behavior. This act is followed by the revelation, to Tashi as well as to the reader, that "*RESISTANCE* IS THE SECRET OF JOY!" (281).

Reading *Possessing the Secret of Joy* is a dual exercise in reading culture. The creator of the fictional world within which the novel's African protagonist lives is an African American woman. As an African who has recently emigrated to the United States with her American husband, Tashi models African Americanness, embodying the culture of Africa and inhabiting the geographical space of the United States. Tashi's body serves as the stage upon which the opera of the relationship between place and ethnic identity can be performed. Both African American women's voices (those of the author and her heroine) are present in the text and confront female circumcision from their various culturally and ethnically embodied spaces. An African and an American, Tashi seems fully aware of the consequences inherent in pledging full allegiance to both, but she is also aware that the two are different—connected but separate. In the novel we get this sense of Tashi's biculturalism from the varying references to her as "Tashi, renamed in America 'Evelyn,'" "Evelyn Johnson," and "Tashi-Evelyn." The names represent her "twoness," the idea of "two souls, two unreconciled strivings; two warring ideals in one dark body" (Du Bois, *Souls* 5); and hers is a struggle to render whole the body torn asunder.

In the collection of essays *In Search of Our Mothers' Gardens,* Walker casts herself as a healer. Her healing efforts are directed to ensure that African women continue to "possess the secret of joy," and thus will be able to pass it on to their diaspora daughters.[4] Athena Vrettos tells us that "by reclaiming the history of black women, those 'creatures so mutilated in body, so dimmed and confused by pain,' and redefining their scars as 'the springs of creativity,'" Walker attempts "to forge spiritual bonds with the past" (455–56). *Possessing* is that attempt. As a cultural fiction, the novel explores how we read others, understand them, and proceed to tell their stories. But it is also about how we—in our understandings of ourselves—are intertwined with the stories we tell. Walker's text explores ethnicity and what it means to possess an ethnic identity.

Possessing the Secret of Joy is the story of two kinds of women: those who are forbidden this possession, the right to own their bodies, and those who forbid others this right. Walker constructs both archetypes: "the mother who betrays" and "the daughter so betrayed" (*Warrior Marks* 21). The conflict is embodied in the relationship between Tashi and M'Lissa. These two women destroy themselves and each other as one adheres to the ritual female circumcision that the other rejects. Alice Walker's novel attempts to mend the bodies torn asunder *and* to reunite those separated by time and space. Thus, Walker's text epitomizes Du Bois's sense of the Negro and the American forming a new being. Importantly, ethnicity is examined as not wholly inherited; rather, it is exposed as "something that is reinvented and reinterpreted" by successive generations (Fischer 195).[5] Ethnicity, then, becomes a fictional space crucial to our understanding. Tashi's narrative shifts from Tashi to Tashi-Evelyn, and her movement between Olinka and the United States emphasizes the relevance of location in the formation of ethnic identity.

Through Tashi, Walker interprets her own ethnicity and demonstrates the importance of its reinvention and redefinition.

Possessing the Secret of Joy critiques myths of culture that sanction and sustain "mutilation" and attempts to recreate for its women subjects a tradition that is liberating and conducive to building strong gendered selves. The characters in this novel are Walker's political mouthpieces; their voices highlight what she considers to be violations of "the blameless vulva" (Dedication). Undoubtedly, the novel demythicizes female circumcision as well as the lives of women who undergo it. Tashi is (re)created, allowed to flourish, if only in her final minutes; Africa is (re)created, as well, but its fate is less kind. Just as Tashi represents the approximately eighty million women who undergo circumcision each year, the village of Olinka stands for the continent of Africa. *Possessing* constructs an Africa where the woman's body serves as the backdrop against which patriarchy is played out. It is this essentializing, totalizing representation that some have found at once objectionable and irresponsible (Wilentz, "Mutilations" 15–16).

While I share some of Gay Wilentz's concerns, I situate *Possessing* within a larger context—Alice Walker's writing life—and I see it as advancing her struggle to know herself. Walker excavates Tashi's history and in the process discovers her own connection to Tashi, blackwoman to blackwoman. Alice Walker uses the writing of *Possessing* as a means of anthropologizing her cultural duality.[6] Indeed, this is a constant in her fiction: she is always in search of her political, social, cultural, gendered self. Using Walker's first novel with a female protagonist as a point of departure and comparison, we can more easily see Tashi as existing on a continuum.[7]

Walker is no idealist when it comes to Africa, nor does she blindly pledge allegiance to Pan Africanist ideology. Her agenda is to figure out how she can take the bitter with the sweet. Though Africa can exist as an integral part of African American awareness of self, Walker reminds us that Africa is distant, and we must always question how we identify with things we see and know from a distance. Walker's cautioning is best summed up by Robert Stepto's assertion that while the identity term *African American* bestows two equal cultural and geographical spaces for locating identity, "it is also a term that cannot help but painfully remind black people in the New World that while they can configure 'America' in increasingly specific, personal terms," the same cannot be designated for "Africa" (xiv). Clearly, the "African" names a space, but "it also teasingly asks us to find it in a haystack as big as a continent" (Stepto xiv). Hence, Walker cannot specify Tashi, for though Tashi is her link, Walker has no specific place to which she can attach herself: "I do not know from what part of Africa my African ancestors came, I claim the entire continent. I suppose that I have created Olinka as my village and the Olinkans as my ancestral tribal peoples" (*Possessing* 285).

Walker has spoken to this longing for a grounding place, a cultural moor-ing site, a "deliberately fixed" place whose "center is where behavior, art, philosophy and language unite as a cultural expression" (Holloway 1). A mooring place is revealed through specified discourse, and sankofa is Walker's discourse of choice. She explains that in attempting to know ourselves through our history, it is important to seek our foremothers and know their works. Walker parallels what Haile Gerima enacts through Mona's transfor-mation, when she posits that "our mothers and grandmothers, *ourselves* have not perished in the wilderness"; but, "we must fearlessly pull out of ourselves and look at and identify with our lives the living creativity some of our great-grandmothers were not allowed to know" (*Mother's Gardens* 235, 237). It is this searching that we see in the characters Dee, Meridian, *The Temple of My Familiar*'s Miss Lissie, and eventually in Tashi.

In "Everyday Use," we find the metaphor for Walker's identity search—that of quilting.[8] This short story explores "heritage," and how it is realized by two black American sisters—Dee and Maggie—through their respective relationships with their mother and grandmother. Dee has developed a fash-ionable attraction to her Southern roots and her African past—she has renamed herself Wangero Leewanika Kemanjo. When asked by her mother, "What happened to 'Dee'?" she replies, "She's dead. I couldn't bear it any longer, being named after the people who oppress me" (418). Ironically, Dee's attempt at connection entails disconnection, since she was named after her grandmother. Dee, with her cosmetic ancestral connection and affected dis-connection, is juxtaposed with Maggie, who is quite fond of her grandmoth-er and is close to her. In the discussion about who should get the quilts, Maggie proclaims: "She can have them Mama, I can remember Grandma Dee without the quilts" (421). Dee's interest in her past is represented by her coveting of ancestral artifacts, namely those quilts made by the woman whose name she bears yet disavows.

Proclaiming her educated awareness of the quilts' cultural, familial, and historical significance, she tells her mother, "Maggie can't appreciate these quilts! She'd probably be backward enough to put them to everyday use" (421). Her mother responds, "She can always make some more. Maggie knows *how* to quilt" (421; emphasis mine). The quilts symbolize history—something of the past to be passed on—but they also symbolize the making of a heritage—quilting as a process. As Gates would have it, quilting represents for Walker "a reassembling of the fragments of [local and] diasporic experience" (*Figures in Black* xxiv). As a novelist, Alice Walker quilts together the bits and pieces of blackwomen's lives and creates a whole that connects them and tells their stories. Though her main emphasis in the essay "In Search of Our Mothers' Gardens" and in this short story is African American women, it was only a matter of time before she branched out into Africa itself. As Gates states more clearly, "[t]o reassemble the fragments of course . . . is to attempt to weave a fiction of origins" (*Figures in Black* xxiv). So, Walker quilts, with Tashi, Maggie, and Meridian supplying related patches.

On the *Meridian:* Walker's Move from Black Women to Blackwomen

In the separate-but-equal South, Meridian has gathered a group of black children for a trip to the circus. However, the day of their visit is not one designated for blacks. Demonstrating her activist inclinations and rebellious spirit, the trip to the circus centers around viewing another rebellious body, "the mummy woman," Marilene O'Shay, who is carted around by her husband and displayed for a fee. The bright banner on the side of the trailer that entombs Mrs. O'Shay announces that "she is one of 12 Human Wonders," while four stars define her as an "Obedient Daughter, Devoted Wife, Adoring Mother, Gone Wrong" (19). For Meridian, this woman represents the shell within which all women are forced to live. The mummy woman symbolizes certain fates experienced by women in general, and by blackwomen in particular. Mrs. O'Shay becomes an embodiment of blackwomanhood as she darkens over the course of her exhibition; efforts by her husband to "paint her original color" fail (20). The mummy woman effects and embodies change; *she* changes. She is a symbol of the fate that will befall women who step outside the boundaries of passive womanness, and her change in color indicates a physiological metamorphosis as well as the results of her immoral ways.

Witnessing the spectacle that Mrs. O'Shay has become, Meridian reflects on her own body as a site of resistance and struggle. Meridian defines her struggle as residing in her resistance to social systems and her search for the inner capacity to change them. This struggle is negotiated through her relationship with her mother. Mrs. Hill is much like the mummy woman, "rigid, static and stifled" (McDowell 266), because she adheres strictly to confining traditions: religion, marriage, and motherhood. Mrs. Hill believes that Meridian stole her freedom, her choices, her spirit, and her chances at revolution. Meridian decides she will not be likewise robbed, and in preparation for her revolutionary role, she returns to the South. Meridian believes that dying for the revolution may be required, and it is a sacrifice she would make. However, though killing for the revolution may be equally necessary, she is ambivalent as to whether she herself can kill. Instead, "perhaps it will be [her] part to walk behind the real revolutionaries—those who know they must spill blood" (201). This spilling of blood parallels Meridian and Tashi, for their revolutionary positions force them to raise the same questions.

Saxon College presents Meridian with restrictive women's roles as the school song declares, "We are as chaste and pure as / the driven snow. / We watch our manners, speech / and dress just so" (93). Meridian breaks these rules when she rescues the "Wile Chile," orphaned, pregnant, and unmarried, and brings her to the college. The tension between tradition and change is deepened when the dean runs the child away, causing her to be struck by a car and killed. The death of the child and the president's refusal to allow Meridian to have her funeral in the school's chapel confirm Meridian's belief that revolution is inevitable—and that only through revolution can she (re)claim the secret joy lost to her mother forever.

The tree Sojourner, on the Saxon campus, embodies Meridian's history. It is all that remains of the plantation that once stood where Saxon College was built; Louvinie, the silenced West African woman, planted this tree. The survival of the tree indicates the sustaining of Meridian's history and heritage.[9] Equally significant, Meridian realizes that her history "extends beyond those around her," beyond the "one life" of black people (women) in the United States.[10] Conjured in the image of the mummy woman and revolutionized in the body of Meridian, Tashi is born. As Alice Walker explores the branches of the tree, the regrown Sojourner, she finds another leaf, wilted and dying. The tree metaphor carries over into *Possessing* and frames our reading of the novel, but it also continues Alice Walker's fictions—and continues her quilting.

The Voice of Heritage, or the Familiar Temple of Tradition

The politics that undergird *Possessing* evidence how the syncretic process of diasporization impacts on literary interpretation, as a mediation on the "cultural presence" in literature (Holloway 12).[11] Karla Holloway reminds us that ethnicity "operates in fictive places in [black texts]; in the imaginative realms, [ethnicity] becomes the ultimate signifier as it plays within the imaginative domains of fictional language" (12). Alice Walker's need for a sistered kinship shapes her construction of Tashi and the Olinkans, and it governs the didacticism of the narrative itself. In addition to this sociopolitical and cultural tradition, Tashi and M'Lissa are characters clearly cast in the African American literary tradition. As Hazel Carby tells us, African American women writers' narratives represent "sufferings and brutal treatment but in a context that is also *the story of resistance*" (*Reconstructing Womanhood* 22; emphasis mine).

Like *Meridian*, *Possessing* is a story of resistance—Alice Walker's resistance to silence and Tashi's resistance to tradition. Furthermore, M'Lissa's indictment epitomizes these resistances. Laurent Jenny tells us that "we can grasp the meaning and structure of a literary work only through its relation to archetypes which are themselves abstracted from a long series of texts" (34). Alice Walker's text is embedded within such a long series, and in order to address this intertextuality, it is necessary that we, as is said in the African American oral tradition, "go to the source."

In *Possessing*, Walker engages several literary traditions. A significant source for reading Walker is Zora Neale Hurston, whose *Their Eyes Were Watching God* is the urtext of contemporary black American women's writing, and of Alice Walker's in particular.[12] While searching for her mothers' gardens, Walker made a trek through the "Garden of the Heavenly Rest" ("Looking for Zora" 304). Among the weeds, Walker discovered what she believes to be Hurston's unmarked grave. An anthropologist by training, Hurston serves as a model for Walker, and one of Hurston's least critically attended works, *Mules and Men,* serves as a model for *Possessing*.

Mules is an artfully constructed collection of fictive folktales that, like *Possessing,* is outfitted with explanatory notes and appendixes.[13] A centralizing folk parable for Walker's text is the brief conversation in the wilderness, which she identifies as a "bumper sticker" and which functions to frame her story the same way the opening tale does in *Mules*. The bumper sticker indicates that *Possessing* is a narrative where someone destroys their own. When we are introduced to Tashi for the first time, she tells us that she is dead, and this realization "reminds [her] of a story" (3). Such frames "purport to assure the [reader] that the fiction is not fictive, not 'parasitic,' but true, or at least based on truth" (Faulkner 333). We are told that "Tashi expressed herself" through stories (*Possessing* 6), so *Possessing,* like *Mules,* is a collection of stories about Tashi and from Tashi herself. The story of her life is surrounded and grounded in folklore and myth to the degree that Tashi herself becomes an embodiment of folklore. While visiting M'Lissa, Tashi learns "that it [is] only the murder of the tsunga, the circumciser, by one of those whom she has circumcised that proves her [the circumciser's] value to the tribe. Her own death, [M'Lissa] declared, had been ordained" (208). When Tashi kills M'Lissa, she reinforces the power she intended to silence and to exterminate.

In Walker's view—and here she differs from Hurston— there is a dark under-side to folklore that impels women to acquiesce in traditions that oppress and repress them.

On her sankofa trek and in an effort to call upon those who have "been ya," Walker begins the interrogation that leads to *Possessing* with *The Temple of My Familiar. Temple* consists of six parts and features a host of characters, but it generally focuses on the life of Miss Lissie, the novel's site of racial memory and "reincarnational shero," and her progeny (Dieke 508). Through Miss Lissie, the novel manifests the ideals of sankofa, first reinvoking the tree metaphor. Miss Lissie explains,

> When you know every branch, every hollow, and every crevice of a tree there was nothing safer; you could quickly hide from whatever might be pursuing you. Besides we shared the tree with other creatures. . . . They seemed nearly unable to comprehend separateness; they lived and breathed as a family, then as a clan, then as a forest, and so on. If I hurt myself and cried, they cried with me, as if my pain was magically transposed to their bodies. (84–86)

With connections to Meridian, Lissie's notions of the tree's ability to provide a hiding place highlight Walker's sankofa-informed writing, revealing the pain of the past, which is shared by all branches of the diaspora tree. As well, Lissie captures the notion of the tree as a site of memory. She explains later that one cannot hide from memory, for to "close the door, a very important door, against memory, against the pain," turns "our very flesh . . . blind and dumb" (352–53). The acknowledgment of the bond of the present to the past heals the violated and offended spirit. Such awakening allows a body to heal and a person to relocate herself in the world, socially, politically, and cultur-ally. This relocation necessitates an ancestor roll call, for "it is against block-age between ourselves and others—those who are alive and those who are dead—that we must work" (353).

The above passage mirrors the intensity felt by Mona and Walker when they entered what remained of slave forts. The entrancing of these temples of the past, too, recalls the novel's title. Miss Lissie recounts a dream that directs our attention to both the title of the novel and its place in Walker's path to Tashi. "Last night I dreamed I was showing you my temple," and thus Miss Lissie goes on to describe her "familiar—what you might these days, unfor-tunately, call a 'pet'—[which] was a small incredibly beautiful creature that was part bird, for it was feathered, part fish, for it could swim and had a somewhat fish/bird shape. . . . Its movements were graceful and clever" (118).

The familiar captures the hybridity of African American existence and manifests the journeys to self that Walker and Mona began as they entered the forts. It is an individual totem and is protective (Dieke 511); it also conflates the sankofa bird and represents Africans' path to the New World. Moreover, the familiar represents the syncretic process of forming diaspora bonds. Entering the temple and recognizing her familiar, the totem that guards her history and her sense of self, Miss Lissie takes the reader to an interior place that symbolizes wholeness, a collective merging of past and present, body and spirit, and the inner order and peace that comes from integrating the past into one's present consciousness, allowing the ancestor to be our guide.

The other characters embody the absence of a sense of history; they capsulize the ways in which the "contemporary social system has little by little begun to lose its capacity to retain its own past, has begun to live in a perpetual present" (Jameson, "Postmodernism" 125). Miss Lissie provides Walker a platform from which to launch further inquiry into her ancestral past and the past of the cultural text she desires to rewrite. Indeed, via Miss Lissie, Walker returns to history, highlights the specific separation of African Americans from their history, and emphasizes the importance not of blind acceptance but of critical engagement with the traditions that history makes available.[14]

With *Possessing,* Walker merges her willingness to engage the voices of those who have gone before and her desire to re/unwrite the problematic cultural texts. Just as Hurston provided an African American literary foundation for Meridian, Walker seeks an African base for Tashi. She engages Flora Nwapa's mild portrayal of circumcision in *Efuru.*[15] Nwapa refers to the operation as a "bath," which in Efuru's case occurs *after* she is married.[16] Buchi Emecheta, considered by many to be the most Western of African women writers, allows circumcision only one line in her *Double Yoke.*[17] Walker does not engage these women writers, who have maintained virtual silence on the subject, with nearly the vigor she brings to male writers who have given free representation to ritual female circumcision. Walker rewrites Ngugi wa Thiong'o's use of circumcision in his novel *The River Between* and Ahmadou Kourouma's in his *The Suns of Independence.*

The former's representation is of utmost significance in reading Tashi's narrative. In *The River Between,* the rite is discussed within the context of the Christian missionaries' arrival and their desire to ban the practice; hence, the community is divided over the continuation of this "sin." For the cultures that support and sustain ritual female circumcision, the practice is quasi-religious.[18] Consequently, Muthoni, Ngugi's female protagonist in *The River*

Between, like Tashi, feels obligated by ethnic solidarity to undergo the rite. Though Muthoni does not physically survive it, she does live long enough to aver that she is a *true* Gikuyu woman. In his *Facing Mount Kenya,* in fact, Jomo Kenyatta, first postcolonial president of Kenya and leader of the Gikuyu, tells us that "irua"—female circumcision—is a "tribal symbol that identifies age-groups" and allows the Gikuyu to maintain and "perpetuat[e] that spirit of collectivism and national solidarity," thus highlighting the necessity of defining ethnicity in relation to place (134; emphasis in original).

Walker's Dura—Tashi's sister who bleeds to death after her operation—is a reembodiment of Muthoni. Kenyatta and Ngugi link the female body to culture and its maintenance.[19] Though both men see the ritual as a tradition whose eradication has the potential to destroy the beauty of Gikuyu tradition and life, Walker critiques the linkage for inspiring the "literal destruction of the most crucial external sign of . . . womanhood: [the] vulva itself" (*Warrior Marks* 21). Indeed, geographic relocation to Walker's United States from a home place likened to Kenyatta's causes Tashi to recognize a new body construction, which in turn reveals that her pleasure and joy have been annihilated. Tashi's confusion informs us that forms of sexuality, as they are defined and experienced, are constituted by the cultural spaces that we inhabit. Changing cultural space affects a (re)construction of sexuality.

Walker's Tashi revises Salimata, the protagonist from Kourouma's *The Suns of Independence.* Salimata does not complete the initiation because she faints, and she is thus caught at the confluence of development: not quite woman but no longer girl-child. Kourouma seems to indict circumcision's status as ritual by likening it to colonial activities that destroyed Africa. Like Tashi, Salimata stands in as a representative woman and as the continent itself. Just as Kourouma allegorizes postcolonial Africa through his character's body, Walker uses Tashi's body as a narrative symbolizing the painful inscriptions that blackwomen's bodies carry, inscriptions that silence them and separate them from each other.

Evidently not content with what she had accomplished in *Possessing,* Walker endeavored to make a documentary film about female circumcision, and as a companion to the film, she published a book cataloging her journey into Africa to make her documentary. In that book, *Warrior Marks: Female Genital Mutilation and the Sexual Blinding of Women,* Walker tells us that *because she* wrote *Possessing,* "there is at least one girl born on the planet today who will not know the pain of genital mutilation. . . . [T]he pen," she says, "will prove mightier than the circumciser's knife" (25). Thus Walker declares that she has found her "mother's garden"—the continent of Africa—and she undertakes sowing her seeds therein. She defines herself a "womanist" and as such is "committed to [the] survival and wholeness of entire people, male and female. Not a separatist, except periodically, for health" (xi). Perhaps *Possessing* is an instance of that "periodi[city]." Chikweyne Okonjo Ogunyemi provides us with an important reading of Walker's womanism. She tells us that "Black womanism celebrates black roots, the ideals of black life while giving a balanced presentation of black womandom" (240). She further suggests that the "ideal" for womanism is "black unity" and that "its aim is the dynamism of the wholeness and self-healing" (240).

Possessing gives voice to the silent diaspora sisters and revises male representations of the ritual as culturally bound. Femaleness for Olinkans is, in part, marked by excision of the clitoris. The women being initiated into that particular cultural nexus are also informed of the sexual boundaries, those involving pleasure and danger: the pleasures of belonging and being defined as Olinkan, and the dangers of sociocultural ostracism and physical death (represented in the text by Dura). Circumcision, then, entails socializing into culture and into sexuality. Walker is trapped in this seemingly immediate space: Can Tashi survive as an alien as Salimata does, between two worlds? Walker's clear response is "no," as evidenced by Tashi's death. Tashi must die after murdering M'Lissa, for her cultural consciousness cannot be separated from her body. The attempt to separate "self from self is quite simply to choose death" (Griffin 231). Walker positions Tashi in a struggle to reconcile her split identity, and her M'Lissa, a cultural icon, establishes that cultural practices that destroy women beget death. However, a tension in the text reveals Walker's own duality. As a womanist, Walker is not only committed to the healing of individual women but also to community healing. Tashi's death symbolizes the degree to which an individual must be sacrificed if damaging cultural practices are to be maintained, and it signifies the danger in foregoing communal wholeness. Furthermore, her death warns women not to rage against the cultural body for the sake of individual rights.

In this sense, Tashi is as guilty of betrayal as the circumciser who violated her. Walker enforces the edicts of wisdom imparted in *Temple*, that the goal of a human's life on earth is to, among other things, "give up their anger" and "forgive . . . every evil done to them" (288–89). Maintained within the confines of these contrasting ideas is the power of Walker's diaspora-conscious voice. Though she is aware of the cultural premises that sustain female circumcision, Walker counters that there is no cultural argument strong enough to justify the "hazardous effects of genital mutilation, not only on health and happiness of individuals, but on the whole society in which it is practiced, and the world" (*Possessing* 285).[20] This position acknowledges a potential dilemma between her womanist consciousness and its concern for community, and her feminist consciousness. Without a doubt, African women have written and spoken out against female circumcision—Walker presents several of them in *Warrior Marks*—but some condemn Walker's analysis as bordering on cultural imperialism, not at all indicating female solidarity.[21] However, Walker forestalls such binary thinking. She foreshadows Tashi's fate in an earlier essay, saying, "[if] we kill off the *sound* of our ancestors, a major portion of us, all that is past, that is history, that is a human being is lost, and we become historically and spiritually thin, a mere shadow of who we were" (*Living by the Word* 62).

Alongside Kourouma's text, Walker's perceivably imperialist sensibilities take on new meaning; they become critiques that aim not to barbarize Africa, but to salvage it from unconscious perpetuation of its own destruction. She suggests that reactionary maintenance of a practice that destroys women will ultimately have dire consequences for nations, cultures, and the continent as a whole. Here, Walker manifests not only her womanist but also her diaspora consciousness. For Kenyatta, Ngugi, and Walker, then, circumcision is about women and the larger issues of national, ethnic, and cultural distinction. Tashi-Evelyn reinforces this view. She responds to questions about her reasons for wanting to be circumcised by averring that it entails "accept[ance] as a real woman by the Olinka people," for "we must keep all of our old ways and no Olinka man—in this [our leader] echoed the great liberator Kenyatta—would even think of marrying a woman who was not circumcised" (122). As the voice from the gallery tells us, women—circumciser and circumcised—hold the primary responsibility for maintaining and perpetuating cultural traditions and mores.

Tashi is, like Alice Walker, an African American woman. Yet Tashi's voice clearly speaks contemptuously of ideas that describe her as a black woman like other black women: "I felt negated by the realization that even my psychiatrist could not see I was African. That to him all black people were Negroes" (18). And when Tashi tells Olivia of her decision to return to Africa to undergo the rite of female circumcision, her description of the latter's response reveals much to the reader about Walker's awareness of her own culturally imperialist tendencies. "Olivia begged me not to go," Tashi says. "But she did not understand. . . . The foreigners were so much more dramatic than Africans dared to be. It made one feel contempt for them" (21). Tashi-Evelyn, when accused of her African self-righteousness and an attitude that conveys the idea that she is "the only African woman to come to America," responds to the charge by admitting it: "I did think this. Black American women seemed so different to me from Olinkan women, I rarely thought of their African great-great-grandmothers" (188). That the African American voice speaks these words becomes highly significant when we consider the double voicedness of Walker's novel. Walker ambitiously aims to construct a conversation that allows her to speak to her African ur-sister and confront their prejudices against each other.

Through Evelyn, Walker attempts to create a nonalien positionality for herself, to connect her voice with those of the African women's collective for whom she speaks through her novel. Tashi, on the other hand, speaks "the word [broken] through to its own meaning and its own expression across an environment full of alien words and various evaluating accents, harmonizing with some of the elements . . . [while] striking dissonance with others" (Bakhtin 277). Walker speaks through Evelyn and establishes her connection to Africa in Tashi's resistance to American influence. Tashi-Evelyn tells us that African women resent African American women because of their brutal honesty: "I was reminded of the quality in African-Americans that I did not like at all. A bluntness. A going to the heart of the matter even if it gave everyone a heart attack" (119). Alice Walker manifests this "going to the heart of the matter" with her exploration of ritual female circumcision, and the "heart attack" is embodied in some Africans' responses to her depiction. Walker anticipates such responses and offers them as part of the narrative itself.

For example, in a chapter that bears her name as title, we find Evelyn on trial for the murder of her circumciser. A woman's voice from the court gallery shouts to Adam, who is in the witness box discussing the ritual, "[t]his is our business you would put into the streets! We cannot publicly discuss this taboo. . . . Your wife has murdered a monument. The Grandmother of the race!" (163). This dramatic intervention demonstrates that Walker is fully aware of the secrecy surrounding the ritual and the political implications involved in relocating it and discussing it publicly. Sassia Singateh reinforces the social significance attached to female circumcision when she says that girls are "given the impression that [they're] going into some glorious experience, relating to womanhood . . . and [they] look forward to that glory" ("Scarred for Life"). With the publication of *Possessing* in 1992, the silence was broken.

Like the dialogue I organize in this text, the most compelling parts of Walker's novel are the sections where Tashi and M'Lissa talk before Tashi kills her. Here the ones whom Walker blames for female genital mutilation—women—are revealed. The relationship between Tashi and M'Lissa is that of

daughter and mother. What informs Walker's manipulation of this relationship, as well as that between Meridian and Mrs. Hill, is the perceived function of mothers in cultural transmission and maintenance. It is from the
women that the girls learn how to identify themselves as women. Meridian
rejects her model; Tashi fights to embrace hers, but she later acquiesces to a
new one, invoking a new female tradition. Nonetheless, M'Lissa, as "custodi-
an of tradition," is key to understanding Tashi's struggle. In order for Alice
Walker to complete her quilting of the lives and struggles of blackwomen, the
bond between these two women must be explored and eventually destroyed.
As Filomena Steady argues, women "represent the ultimate value" for African
lives, "the continuity of the group" (32). Hence, it is necessary that modeled
behaviors encourage holistic sustenance.

In *Our Own Freedom,* Buchi Emecheta photographically explores "mothers handing down the future to their daughters" (47). Alice Walker questions
the tradition that Emecheta's mothers pass on, and she posits the daughter's
right to refuse those traditions that physically and spiritually scar her. We
have seen with Meridian that blackwomen's daughters can choose, but these
choices come at a high cost—their own alienation. Alice Walker wants us to
believe that every woman has choices. The mothers of blackwomen have the
freedom to choose the traditions to which they will adhere and that they will
ultimately transmit to their daughters. Because the establishment of this freedom is central to Walker's mission, she has created an alternate tradition for
her diaspora sisters, one wherein women are informed by the past, educated
in the present, and led by each other into a transformed future of "global
communal harmony" (Braendlin 55).

In *Warrior Marks,* Walker defines herself as "a great believer in solidarity,"
and I am certain it was this belief that precipitated the journey of writing
Possessing the Secret of Joy. Tashi's story begins much like Meridian's. Tashi tells
us, "I did not realize for a long time that I was dead" (1). We accompany
Tashi on a quest that gives her life—even in her actual death. We discover
that tradition—embodied by women and disembodying women—has affected Tashi's death. But there are other traditions affecting Tashi, as well. One is
Christianity, against which she—like Meridian and Shug and her followers in
Temple—rebels. Like Meridian, Tashi is a revolutionary. She rejects the rigid
God of the Judeo-Christian tradition and embraces a new God, the Olinka
leader who is called Jesus Christ. But with this embrace she is engaged in
another revolution, against another tradition.

In order to fulfill her revolutionary mission, Tashi must relocate to Olinka
land, to Africa, just as Meridian returns to the South to find herself, to

emerge anew. Tashi must discover the tree from which she branches out. Tashi, "the grownup daughter," returns to receive "the only remaining stamp of Olinka tradition" (64). "The operation [she wanted to have done to her] joined her, she felt, to [Olinkan] women, whom she envisioned as strong, invincible. Completely woman. Completely African. Completely Olinka" (64). The operation inscribes Tashi into the history of her people. But it is this inscription that confines and restricts her life. Like the mummy woman, she is expected "to lay back and *be* pleasured" (*Meridian* 20).[22]

Reading African Women While Writing Herself: Walker's Web

Possessing is a significant phase in Walker's intellectual and creative sankofa journey. As a cultural fiction, *Possessing* engages the cultural reality wherein the "'black' psyche in America" ("Brotherhood" 28) meets the African psyche, and it endeavors to join the two psyches, to unite their struggles toward freedom. Walker engages the gendered psyche of an African woman, and attempts to rewrite a tradition. There are strong biases in Walker's reading of Africa and in her presentation of the particulars of ritual female circumcision. Walker clearly recognizes those prejudices that are enabling, but she fails to fully engage those that hinder. For this, she will undoubtedly always be criticized. Remarkably, though, Walker has managed, in spite of herself, to write a novel journey into the black gendered self. In endeavoring to give voice to Tashi, she has "uncovered" a significant point of contention in black American identity politics. Walker masks her personal struggle in the garb of an African woman's fight for sexual and spiritual freedom. As an author, Walker functions as a vehicle for "characteriz[ing] the existence, circulation and operation of certain discourses in society" (Foucault, *Language* 124). The discourse she has informed and in many ways perpetuated and questioned is that of African American ethnicity.

Rachel Blau DuPlessis tells us that "one of the great moments of ideological negotiation in any work occurs in the choice of resolution" (3). The spiritual bond that Walker has forged with Tashi ends when Tashi dies. This is indeed a most problematic portion of the text. Why does Tashi have to physically die, just when she is spiritually reborn? In telling the "untold tale" of an African woman's trauma, Walker designs a story that cannot but outrage even the most disinterested reader. Yet Walker has woven a web of conflict into her tale that critiques and offers resistance to her most cherished beliefs. She speaks at one and the same time as a person of African descent who maintains what many term a Western imperialist position that requires that the Other change.

Possessing the Secret of Joy is political: Tashi is not woman but symbol, a symbol of the old acquiescence to patriarchal victimization. However, she is both victim and victimizer. Her decision to comply with traditions that debase women renders her guilty, an accomplice who must suffer for not knowing, on her own, that ritual female circumcision *is* mutilation. But I wonder if there is no "safe haven" for women who suffer as Walker's Tashi does. I suspect that there is, but the culture of Alice Walker does not allow us access to discourses that license such "safe havens," and for Walker a life postcircumcision is death. Walker is of her place, and she can only write her self, even while writing Tashi as that self. If Tashi were to survive, then she would transmit another tradition of resistance/resilience: ritual female circumcision does not scar the individual human will to survive. But this is not Walker's message. Walker replaces the Olinka myths and archetypes with a new prototype: the bare-bottomed screaming girl babies. These new voices cry for their physical, spiritual, and sexual freedoms. They represent African American women's desire to be freed from damaging diaspora bonds and forge in this land new rituals for survival and identity. Unlike Tashi, their cause will be their own survival. These bodies are conceived of as Western, "bounded, unique, more or less integrated" individuals (Geertz 229). Tashi becomes the sacrificial lamb, as it were. Her death is necessitated by a social agenda and a political program: she must die so that Walker can kill the tradition Tashi embodies.

This poses a sankofa moment for me, as well, as I am taken back to the narrative of *Temple,* wherein Walker aims to accentuate Afracentric wisdom. Walker's fictional mask is adorned with a nonfictional, political purpose. Tashi and M'Lissa both, before their deaths, decry a tradition to which they had previously steadfastly held. Yet these two manipulated and pitiful women, so grossly controlled by their author, deserve no fate smaller than death. The illusion that Walker would create, however, is that we *should* care for them, that her concern is for Tashi. My objection to such posturing is that Tashi is cast as secondary to Walker's political agenda, and the message the novel sends about African women is inconsequential. Though the *Gospel According to Shug,* as we are given it in *Temple,* stresses the importance of forgiveness, Walker does not forgive M'Lissa, and she makes no narrative intervention, through tone or style (Strong-Leek 197–99). Though Walker realizes that Tashi, and M'Lissa to a lesser degree, have their own voices, she commands those voices and constructs a conversation that is more with herself. She does not hear her sisters or heed their voices. Here, Alice Walker shows the weakness in her diaspora consciousness. She has yet to cross the diaspora divide; her sankofa journey is not yet complete.

Trinh T. Minh-ha correctly maintains that when an "us"/"them" conversation takes place, with "us" being the West, the conversation becomes "rather intimate: a chatty talk, which, under cover of cross cultural communication, simply superposes one system of signs over another" (68). The raising of the crying babies clearly replaces Tashi's silent pangs and nightmares. Tashi cannot speak her pain; she dreams her suffering and endures in silence. Deprived of the power of utterance, Tashi cannot say but is said. Walker creates a fiction grounded in American discourses of racial, cultural, and gendered connectedness. She writes herself an African woman, a sister who can speak her thoughts, legitimize her politics, and ingratiate herself with those to whom she is historically connected. She has created a kinship that, though in some ways functional, is nevertheless unilateral. There is no interrogation of the dimensions of Tashi's being beyond those resulting from the sexual/physical manipulation that Walker sees. She attempts to come to terms with her sisters on a level of solidarity that she would claim is spiritual but in the end seems sexual. Unfortunately, in her attempt to speak for female solidarity and to raise world consciousness about crimes against women, Walker forgets to listen to those Other voices and hear their direction. Neither Tashi nor Alice Walker fully interrogate the complexities of Tashi's cultural being, class, or otherwise. Though she has answered the call of the sankofa bird and heeded its warning, Walker still has no integrated sense of what her African past means, how she should incorporate it into her recent sense of herself as a "African AmerIndian woman." In many ways, Walker, both in her fictional character Tashi and in her own expressed beliefs, manifests the localized African American condition: an inability to see beyond color and beyond race, which is the terminal fate of those marked by and with a double consciousness.

Nonetheless, Walker opens the door for a critique of her representations that requires her readers to first reconcile the various textual voices, the articulated and muted ideologies. In this vein, she welcomes a response from her diaspora sisters, which informs her own sense of their kinship while exposing the difficulties of such bonding. Particularly, Walker draws our attention to the most glaring of *Possessing*'s muted ideologies—class. Circumcision marks a class of women, a boundary between the acceptable and the unacceptable. Moreover, Tashi, as Olinkan, and Olivia, as African American, are separated by class, as well. The former represents the newly emigrated and yet to be integrated American, while Olivia has citizenship privilege. Furthermore, Tashi and M'Lissa occupy different classes in that M'Lissa is represented as an uneducated bush woman who fails because she has not yet been enlightened, but

Tashi's ideological and physical exposure to the West has socially advanced her. Walker does not engage this class dynamic, for her inquiry is exclusively gender- and color/race-driven. However, in Michelle Cliff's work, the interpretive flow of double consciousness is interrupted with the introduction of a new color semantic. Cliff also makes an understanding of how race and color—related but distinct—and place interrelate to form a significant aspect of any attempt at kinship.

chapter three

"Dis here is fe me territory": White Sand, Blue Water, and Cliff's Space for the Creole

The question that introduced the opening chapter, "What is Africa to me?" is not an exclusively black American inquiry. From the Caribbean, Derek Walcott, in his poem "A Far Cry from Africa," poses the dilemma thus: "Where shall I turn, divided to the vein?" (18). Wherever a population of dispersed Africans resides, the issue of Africa's place in their identity surfaces, along with spirited debate. As well, their specific location frames their debate. In any discussion of the African diaspora, attention to the Caribbean is as inevitable as it is complicated. While in the United States, the destructive binaries of racist and sexist discourses are delineated in a diaspora politic of kinship like Alice Walker's, it is otherwise in the Caribbean, where intersections of nation, race, and identity are more entangled. Walker's is a politic grounded in a theory of race, whereas racial identity in the Caribbean is complicated by the presence of what Judith Raiskin calls "the third term," Creoleness (xi).

This complication is captured in Jeanne Garane's explication of "the problem of West Indian ancestry." She writes that many so-called West Indian nations, "born collectively of imperialist aggression," are rejected by both Africa and Europe; therefore, their "is(le)olation" forces "West Indians [to] search for an independent identity looking neither to Europe nor to Africa, but to a West Indian past," in effect creating a history (155). Garane both highlights the fictional quality of identity and points out the peculiarities of the Caribbean in particular. Where most early Caribbean fiction focuses on the relationship between colony and mother country, Cliff inserts the United States into her politic, making her writing particularly useful in an analysis of diaspora consciousness.[1] Like Walker's Tashi, Cliff's Clare manifests a politic affected by relocation. Before turning to Cliff's *Abeng* and *No Telephone to Heaven*, however, we will examine the book considered by many to be the first English-speaking Caribbean woman's narrative: Mary Prince's *History of Mary Prince, A West Indian Slave, Restated by Herself.*

Prince's autobiography underscores Walker's elision of class and provides a lens through which we can see the intersections between color and class in both a Creole and a diaspora consciousness (the former grounded in physical morphology, the latter in history). Prince consistently refers to free mulatto women in negative terms. In one specific instance, her anger toward them for abusing their bodily/color privilege is obvious: "Mrs. Wood . . . hired a mulatto woman. . . . I thought it very hard for a coloured woman to have rule over me because I was a slave and she was free. . . . The mulatto woman was rejoiced to have power to keep me down. . . . there was no living for the slaves—no place after she came" (204). This uneasy relationship between free and slave recasts Du Bois's "problem of the color line." As the excerpt from Prince shows, it is not so much the fact of the new nurse's color as it is her disposition that is disturbing. She aims to use her status as a means to oppress her darker and enslaved sisters. Similar to the concept of race in African America, the notion of Creole infuses the literature of the Caribbean. Raiskin, in fact, posits that "'Creoleness' can be understood both as evidence of particular political histories and nationalist movements and as an ongoing practice of articulating those histories in the languages of the people they have shaped. . . . [Such articulations turn] attention away from the body to consciousness" (5).

Mary Prince's experiences in the marginalized Caribbean spaces of Bermuda, Turks Island, and Antigua foreground issues in Cliff's *No Telephone to Heaven*. Clare, the main character, claims a narrative voice in herstory. As a non-Creole, Prince provides an outsider's insight into the psyche manifest in Clare Savage. Clare's body and consciousness are merged into a representational narrative of Creole subjectivity. Cliff's protagonist journeys and crosses "racial," geographical, and social boundaries.[2] Clare's "political radicalism" is not representative of Cliff's "fashionable attitude," but comes "accompanied by profound insights into the experimental nature of the arts" (W. Harris, "Tradition" 46).

Cliff experiments with the intersections between fictional genres in ways that provide the "profound insights" that Harris finds absent in earlier West Indian fiction. Specifically, in her first two novels, Cliff takes the traditional form of the *bildungsroman* and transforms its "individualistic bourgeois quest plot into a collective struggle for social justice" (Barnes 23). In *No Telephone to Heaven*, Cliff infuses her vision of the *bildungsroman* with an interrogation of the documentary film genre, which revises both fiction and history in its attempts to represent the relationship between place and identity. In much the same way, *Sankofa* exposes the connections between place and sense of self through Mona's translocation in place and time, and Walker relocates herself to Africa to simultaneously document a historical and physical trauma of ritual female circumcision and respond to the historical challenge the ritual poses to her as a descendant of circumcised women. In both Walker's and Cliff's inquiries, the camera becomes an eye that sees history and place as connected and projects the understanding of that connection onto the screen of blackwomen's cultural development. Cliff further develops Walker's linking of history and place.

In both *Abeng* and *No Telephone to Heaven,* narratives of Clare Savage's becoming, Cliff constructs a radical narrative style that merges Barbara Harlow's notion of "resistance literature" with what Frederic Jameson terms "national allegory" ("Third World Literature" 69). In her analysis of post-independence African narratives, Harlow suggests that resistance literature not only "calls attention to itself" but also situates itself firmly in the "struggle against ascendant and dominant forms of ideological and cultural production" (28–29). This *littérature engagée*[3] corresponds to Jameson's ideas about so-called Third-World literature and its inherent political foci.[4] Within the gap between Harlow's and Jameson's assessments, Cliff enjoys a favorable position: she makes national allegory individual as well as sociopolitical. That is, the narrative forces us to weigh the effects of politics, yet her characters escape becoming symbolic victims of that political behavior.[5] In *No Telephone to Heaven,* Cliff uses an interrogation of the documentary film genre to highlight the intersections of fiction and history, between place and identity.

Michelle Cliff engages in a debate about history, representation, and identity, revising the context within which, and the terms by which, we understand Caribbean diaspora experience. Using diaspora consciousness as a theory of positionality and reading Cliff's writings through it, I suggest that identity, as encoded in terms of color, class, history, and place, is like a language. Cliff's queries assume the syntax of the traditional novel but infuse this form with a narrative voice that challenges the novel as capable of containing its story. The "middle passage," that vast consuming sea of/from history, directs both Cliff and Walker. However, Walker's reading encircles her because of her own ancestral, physical, and spiritual link with Tashi, both as fiction and as historical artifact. Yet Cliff's reading navigates the landscapes of history, memory, and myth, creating an allegory that embodies an alternative history—one that is not necessarily conflicting with Walker's but one that revises hers through the logic of her Creoleness.

In *Claiming an Identity They Taught Me to Despise,* Cliff excavates historical memory as it relates to identity. Because she is diaspora conscious, the narration in this text is necessarily migratory; she must come to understand the complicated relations that make her what she is. This narrative begins in Jamaica and moves to the United States, a movement that reflects Cliff's own birth and early rearing in Jamaica and her adulthood in the United States. She tells us: "I and Jamaica is who I am. No matter how far I travel—how deep the ambivalence I feel about returning. And Jamaica is a place in which we/they/I connect and disconnect—change place" (76). Cliff's work actively engages the relationship between heritage, gender, and location in the ascription of identity. I offer that the "we/they/I" to which Cliff refers are respectively people of African, English, and Creole descent. The separated connection of these identities by slashes indicates that for Michelle Cliff the identity is building: African past meets the colonial English, yielding the creole writing subject. Cliff's "I" is (included in) both "we" and "they," and these subject pronouns indicate connection and disconnection.

In her prose poem "The Laughing Mulatto (Formerly a Statue) Speaks," Cliff's narrator, who is "writing the story of [her] life as a statue," laments that her creator had not carved her "from the onyx of Elizabeth Catlett. Or molded me from the dark clay of Augusta Savage. Or cut me from mahogany or cast me in bronze." She wishes she were "dark plaster like Meta Warrick's Talking Skull" rather than the "white marble of no homeland" (*Land of Look Behind* 85). The references to black women artists demonstrate the narrator's identification with their art as a way of locating herself.[6] But her understanding of herself, her vision of herself, as homeless, "a figure of no homeland," is also particularly significant within the context of sistered kinship. The notion of homelessness recalls a lack of roots resulting from erased historical memory and loss of connectedness. As well, this desire to be "dark plaster" captures the issues of color that torment the characters in *Abeng*.

Coming Home to History: Scripts of Culture as/in Fiction

After studying in England, Clare returns to Jamaica and encounters "a past that is [her] own country reterritorialized, even terrorized, by another" (Bhabha, "In a Spirit" 329). The terror Clare meets is embodied in the presence of an American film crew embarking on a cinematic production based on the life of the legendary Maroon woman warrior Nanny. That the filmmakers have chosen a Maroon as their subject is particularly telling, for as Barbara Lalla notes, "Maroon heritage in Jamaica has always been, in many ways, a subtext to imperial history . . . and elicits a reading of the past that is cumulative and intertextual" (186). The making of the film is the occasion for Clare's involvement with the resistance, and her own attempt to (re)make Jamaica (as) a possible homeland. Just as Gerima's *Sankofa* aptly frames *Possessing* as Walker's journey into diaspora history, this documentary about Jamaica's mother frames Cliff's sankofa inquiry, as well.

Walker's creation of Tashi is informed by a womanist compulsion and a Western sense of her historical bind; Gerima's Mona shows a parallel sense of diaspora linkages. However, the appearance of film in Cliff's novel highlights how, for Cliff, home is a social place whose history must be narrated and (re)presented according to local understandings. In the case of Nanny's narrative, Jamaicans must control her representation, for she is their national mother, an affirmation of some aspect of their existence.

Within this frame, the film represents a "fake archaeology of history," providing a comfortable version of the past that is palatable for mass culture consumption, a way of "*reprogramming* popular memory" (Foucault, "Film and Popular Memory" 25). Clare and her band of revolutionaries realize that it is "necessary to confront [this reprogramming] with a genuine archaeology. Their popular memory of struggle—which has never really found expression, never had the power to do so—must be refreshed, faced with forces that are constantly striving to stifle it, and silence it for good" (25). The genuine archaeology the novel provides, however, is not solely that of Nanny, but of Jamaica, and as such Clare advances Walker's Meridian. While both are willing to give their lives to become agents of social and cultural change, Clare is also willing to kill, which marks her as a full-fledged revolutionary.

At one point in the novel, we find Clare traveling in the back of a pickup truck with other revolutionaries, bound for armed conflict at the filming location and ready to disrupt the Western attempt to cannibalize Jamaica's "indigenous history and culture" (Barnes 25). The word *cannibalize* is deliberately chosen for its historical resonance: *cannibal* is a corruption of *Carib*, referring to those who offered the fiercest resistance to colonization, and thus compelling the colonizer to cast them in the direct terms of savagery. Cannibalizing Jamaica, the film also returns us to *The History of Mary Prince*. Her narrative is filtered through the pen of the amanuensis and the scrutiny of editor Thomas Pringle. The prefatory material informs us that though the narrative was "written out fully," it was "pruned . . . , retaining as far as was practical Mary's exact expression and peculiar phraseology" (45). These notions of "practical" retentions and "pruning" undergird the revolutionary resistance to the conversion of Nanny's life into digestible film drama. As Prince alerts us to the limits of autobiography, so the film signals limits of biography—Tashi's, Mona/Shola's, and Nanny's—through a European filter.

Cliff speaks to the question of historical narrative in her novel *Free Enterprise,* where she addresses the same issues we find in the historical, sociological, and creative writings of Orlando Patterson and Edward Kamau Brathwaite from the 1960s and early 1970s. As Brathwaite suggests, "history becomes anthropology and sociology, psychology and literature and archaeology, whatever else is needed to make the fragments whole" (22). In *Free Enterprise,* Cliff attempts to make whole the fragmented consciousness of African diaspora women in her depiction of Annie Christmas, a Jamaican creole woman of privilege who leaves the luxury of her middle-class life to fight for the abolitionist cause. Much like Clare Savage, Annie Christmas identifies revolt against America's notion of "free enterprise" as necessary to having a life that is relevant. Christmas resigns herself to Carville, a leper colony in Louisiana, and Cliff carefully parallels the existence of lepers with that of people caught in the tangles of creole and diaspora history.

In the context of my analysis, leprosy, a disease of the skin, makes a peculiarly fitting analogy for the issue of color that haunts Clare. Moreover, the treatment of lepers provides a parallel for the colonization of Caribbean spaces like Jamaica. It becomes Clare's mission to resist the further co-opting of Jamaican territory by the appropriations of Nanny's story as national mother. As well, Annie Christmas recognizes the importance of stories and of possessing narrative power. In the chapter titled "Oral History," we find Annie interrogating these narratives that conscript lepers as disruptive nuisances, exiled because they "threatened the common good" (*Free Enterprise* 45). People who were sent away to colonies like the one she inhabits were significantly described as being "in the silence," their presence not erased, but muted. This muting allows, however, for a narrative to be spoken *about* them, similar to Walker's speaking for African women through Tashi. It is this place "in the silence" between muting and erasing that Clare Savage wants to fill with Nanny's voice and a story less colorful than the filmmakers have designed, for Clare, like Cliff herself, suspects that "the truth lies somewhere in between" the fiction of the film and the [local] memory of the history (51). Clare's mission is one not so much of retrieving History, but of retrieving personal history, for "the official version entertains. Illumines the Great White Way" (17).

The struggle at the center of *No Telephone* is over the power to narrate, interpret, and (re)present Jamaica's history. Beyond challenging the American gaze, the novel speaks to a fixing of Caribbean history in the prism of the camera. Cliff likewise resists inscription of the Caribes as exotic in their primitiveness and savagery. The eye of the camera focuses on the disparity between civilization and savagery, consolidating a history of Jamaican representation. In this instance, however, the gaze both civilizes and uncivilizes the savage, manifesting a cinematic stasis in which the dynamic Nanny becomes one-dimensional (W. Harris, *Kas-Kas* 47–48). Hence, the logic for the resistance is that Jamaica has been "turned to stage set too much" (121). The resisters are revolting against the film's history as well as its commodification of Jamaica as a mythic paradise, recalling the travel poster that advertises "JAMAICA, A WORLD OF CULTURE WITHOUT BOUNDARIES" (6). They aim to prevent attempts by tourists and others to "Make [Jamaica their] own" (187).

The Jamaica in Cliff's narrative is neither without boundaries nor allowed to coexist alongside its American mythology. Cliff challenges the American mistake of "lumping the islands together, with an ignorant familiarity, as though they were indistinct places, sharing history and custom, white sands and blue waters indiscriminately" (*No Telephone* 64). Using its reality as a complex land split by class and color, Cliff erases the vision of a vacation paradise, and the American presence becomes a commercial and violent one.

Joining in her mother's resentment at the conflation of the islands into one, Clare rejects the romanticization of Nanny's life. An enigmatic figure, Nanny has existed in Jamaican consciousness without the solidity of flesh or blood the actress in the film gives her. Was she an Ashanti priestess who kept the whites at bay for years as she led a liberation resistance, or was she a creature of legend who could "catch a bullet between her buttocks" (*Abeng* 7)? The issue of Nanny's historical reality and her fate again returns us to Cliff's *Free Enterprise,* but this time our attention is focused on Mary Ellen Pleasant. A restaurateur, Pleasant supplies the funds for John Brown's failed raid, yet her epitaph reads simply "A Friend of John Brown." The power of her wealth becomes mysterious legend: "Who has ever heard of Mary Ellen Pleasant?" (16). Like Nanny, this revolutionary blackwoman in the struggle for black liberation is encoded in a narrative of "voodoo queen, mammy, whore, and savagery" (20). The similar fates of the Jamaican and African American women signal Cliff's embrace of the diaspora connections, yet the contrast in their local prominence underscores the politics of place.

Free Enterprise takes its title from Pleasant's restaurant, the site of the meetings that culminated in her financial and historical contribution to black liberation. In like fashion, *No Telephone to Heaven* takes its title from the sign painted on the truck that transports Clare and her band of revolutionaries: "No voice to God. A waste to try. Cut off. No way of reaching out or up. Maybe only one way. Not God's way. . . . NO TELEPHONE TO HEAVEN.

The motto suited them. Their people. The place of their people's labor. So lickle [*sic*] movement in this place. From this place. Then only back and forth, back and forth, over and again, over and again, for centuries" (15–16). The guerrillas' motto emphasizes the inability of the natives to resist continued American efforts to (over)write their history. In her short story collection *The Store of a Million Items,* Cliff makes the resistance to American imperialism more explicit. Jamaica is defined by "the appearance of something in The Store of a Million Items," which promised "a bounty only available" through "transactions" with America (42, 2). Like the traveling salesman in "Transactions," who "travels into the interior of the island, his car packed with American goods," the film feeds America's desire to own Jamaica, to satisfy the Jamaicans' "love [for] things American," while simultaneously representing the diverging perspectives of the location itself (*Store* 4). A scene from the film evidences the dissonant representations. The narrator points out the contrast between the actress who plays Nanny, dressed in "a pair of leather breeches and a silk shirt," and the historical record of her "as an old woman naked except for a necklace made from the teeth of whitemen" (260).

Furthering emphasizing the dilemma of American-Jamaican relations, Clare and the renegades can critique the set-designed clothing of their indigenous hero, but they do so in a theatrical dress of their own. In their efforts to reclaim Jamaica and resist American commodification and exploitation of Jamaican culture, history, and economy, they are equipped with black market American weapons exchanged for Jamaican marijuana. Their surplus camouflage jackets have the names of American soldiers still attached—"and they called each other by the name on the pockets: Johnson, Washington, Skroboski, Dias, Morrisey" (7). Their own costumes reveal their vicarious association with America the power they are resisting, and added "a touch of realism, cinematic *vérité,* that anyone would believe they were faced with *real* soldiers. True soldiers—though no government had ordered them into battle—far from it. But this is how the camouflage made them feel" (7). Not only are the renegades at home in their camouflage, but they don it to protect their home. The camouflage is a mask, an attempt to pass as Americans, inviting and invited into the Jamaican landscape. But their masks hide their revolutionary impulses and cover as dual strategy: Clare "must make [herself] visible," yet passing "demands a desire to become invisible" (*Land of Look Behind* 19, 21). The costumes become necessary to claim the space that is their own.

Clare's claim is national as well as personal. Critical to her adoption of a revolutionary stance is her genealogical linkage to Nanny. Her grandmother

Inez was a descendant, on her father's side, from the "Maroons, Ashanti from the Gold Coast" (*Abeng* 33). Maroon heritage is distinctly "restorationist," focused on perpetuating traditions that emphasize freedom and selfhood (Campbell 13). So, though Clare engages in a revolt and likens herself to a revolutionary, her aim is to restore Nanny, resist her inscription through "the white filter of the official version" (*Free Enterprise* 7). Thus, her objective is twofold: to challenge the official version of Nanny and that of Jamaica as well.

Gordon Lewis, in his *The Growth of the Modern West Indies,* argues that the "insularism" that defines the Caribbean is "the basic responsibility" of Great Britain and the English, "who kept the islands unnaturally apart from each other for three centuries or more and then expected them to come together" (18). The notion of an integrated and unified Caribbean problematizes the notion of identity in ways particularly poignant in the context of diaspora consciousness. Identity, here, implies both the manifestation of a vision and a unity of purpose that transcends micronationalist politics and the no less political notion of individual subjectivity and self-placement in the macrocosm of the world stage. The former engages what Ali Mazrui terms cultural engineering, the constructing of institutions and ideologies that will enable new nations to embark on nationhood with integrity and a sense of purpose. He writes that "Cultural engineering becomes the deliberate manipulation of cultural factors for the purposes of deflecting human habit in the direction of new and perhaps constructive endeavors . . . [or] changing cultural patterns enough to make it possible for certain institutions to survive . . . [or] basically attitudinal change" (xv). Though Mazrui speaks specifically of East Africa, I note similarities between the regions that allow me to apply his ideas here.[7] Unlike the displaced African who resides in the United States, where, theoretically at least, a culture of difference makes a holistic identity possible, the Caribbean is seasoned with differences that constitute individually constructed cultures.

Geographically, the Caribbean is multinationed, with each nation being a site of particular cultural fashioning. Mazrui identifies two major foci in his analysis: writing of history and creative literature. Through Michelle Cliff's "logic of a creole," this cultural engineering and its requisite attention to a diaspora politic becomes Clare Savage's mission. Though the United States is seen as aggressor and threat, the boundary-less Jamaica, locked "in the silence," has developed a vocal and defensive border structured by its memory of history and a resistance to its distortion.

As Cliff indicates in "Make It Your Own," Jamaicans resent the implication that America put it on the map, and that resentment manifests itself in a wish that they "could destroy [the American tourist enterprise] without destroying" Jamaica (*Land of Look Behind* 84). Disguised as Americans, Clare and her renegades fight for a Jamaica that has become, for her, a significant space, perhaps the place she could (finally) call home.

The idea of "home" figures centrally in Clare's journey in search of her own space and how she would come to place herself within it. Carole Boyce Davies states that "home becomes a critical link in the articulation of identity" (*Black Women* 115); some would argue that it is in many ways analogous to it. Critical to understanding the alienation and isolation Cliff and her novel's protagonist Clare Savage articulate and experience, bell hooks profoundly suggests that "at times home is nowhere. At times one only knows extreme estrangement and alienation. Then home is not just one place. It is locations" ("Choosing the Margin" 148). Davies explores a related idea in the form of "migrations of self" and argues that for "postcolonial" women subjects, migration is a means of locating identity. However, in the tradition established by the writers I read, Clare travels through hooks's "home is nowhere" to find that Jamaica is where home *can be*.

In *Abeng*, alongside the history of Jamaica, we are given the history of the Savages, Boy, Kitty, and their two daughters, Clare and Jenny. The novel takes its title from the African word meaning "conch shell." Historically, the shell functioned as a means of communication in Africa. In Jamaica, and elsewhere in the Caribbean, the conch shell served to summon the slaves to the fields, to sound out calls of rebellion, to announce death, and to transmit messages among escaped slaves, or Maroons. The abeng as an African agent of sound becomes in Jamaica a mark of fracture and resistance (Gikandi 237). The dual usage of the abeng parallels Jamaican double consciousness, and it embodies female rebellion through its womblike configuration. Hence, it is evidence of Clare's connection to a displaced African past lost under the sea and her functional distance from it. The abeng serves to reconstitute memory of a past history.[8] Cliff defines Clare Savage as a "crossroads character" mirroring the duality of the abeng: as the child of a Freeman and a Savage. Moreover, the symbolism of these lexemes infuses a historical dimension to Clare's experiences, as well, for "freeman" connotes those who were once savage but are now tamed, while "savage" has connotations that require no explanation.

Though her ancestry is racially mixed on both sides, this merging is interpreted to and for Clare in significantly different ways, and it is these divergent representations that color Clare's experiences. Clare's father, James Arthur "Boy" Savage, fashions his ancestry through the 1829 arrival of his

English great-grandfather "James Edward Constable Savage, the puisne justice and advisor to the Crown" (*Abeng* 29). Judge Savage owned a large plantation that housed one hundred slaves, all of whom he murdered on the eve
of emancipation. Having left a wife in England, Judge Savage, according to
family mythology, was "one of the only Jamaican landowners never to
impregnate a female slave or servant—that is not to say, of course, that he
never raped one" (*Abeng* 29). Though he took a "mistress" who was half
Miskito Indian and half African, she was modified in the family lore to "part
Indian and part Spanish" (*Abeng* 30). This "personification of the New
World" bore a son, J. A. C. (Jack) Savage, who drank away most of the family fortune. Jack married Isabel Frazier, "a woman of similar background,"
and they had five daughters and one son. Their social background is powerful, for this, too, is a mixed-race marriage, with Isabel merely passing for
white (*Abeng* 41).

While Jack speaks of similarity in class and social terms, he is unaware of
the extent to which they are truly similar; they are both, unbeknownst to
each other, passing. While Jack assumes their histories are similarly white, the
reader is fully cognizant of the slippage in their ancestries, and knows that
their actual similarity is in parallel erasure of blackness. "Boy" was born to
Jack Savage's second-youngest daughter Caroline. Being "high yaller," she
performed in New York City in a production of "Shuffle Along" (*Abeng* 41),
until she met the "iceman from Sicily," with whom she had Boy.[9]

Ever aware of her role as a Savage, Caroline "could not marry beneath her
'station,'" so she "invented" a death for her lover and "faced up to her fate,"
recalling that "some of the greatest men in history had been bastards" (*Abeng*
41). After the birth, she sends the "boy" to live with her sister in Harbour
Town, accompanied by a Jamaican girl returning home. This episode outlines
not only Caroline's respect for her family's class affiliation, but also her con-
currence with the tendency of Savages to construct family history, a legacy
that conscripts Boy as he remains true to it. Raised by his alcoholic aunt and
uncle until he leaves for boarding school, Boy clings to the mythology of his
whiteness and the privilege that it endows. Though he loves the black and
white Creole Jesuit priests who handle his education and who teach him "to
respect elitism," he nonetheless trades "their Catholicism for Calvinism"
(*Abeng* 45). He is fascinated by the "concept of the Elect—those whose names
were recorded before time. . . . The ones who had been chosen" (*Abeng* 46).
And he is sure that when the record is unsealed "his name would be revealed
alongside the names of other Savages," and he takes pride in this conception
of himself. Clinging to his family's "former wealth," Boy adopts the

additional legacy of "an arrogance which seemed to grow in relation to [the Savages'] losses," and he sets "out to earn no [other] distinctions at all" (*Abeng* 29, 45).

He meets and marries Kitty Freeman, though her family does not approve. Unlike the Savages, the Freemans have no mythology of whiteness that defined their family, no creed of color that bound and entitled them. Yet they too are landowners and "red people" (*Abeng* 38). Although Boy, "lost in a myth which [he] believed," assures Clare that regardless of her mother's obviously colored ancestry, "she is white because [she is] a Savage," Kitty infuses Clare's life with "a sense of Jamaica that [Boy] would never have" (*Abeng* 52). Kitty's efforts to instill this place include trips to the country, frequent travel from "St. Elizabeth to Kingston, bringing back to town things from the country, and bringing to the country things from town. These two distinct places created the background for the whole of their existence" (*Abeng* 49). Kitty has a reverence for things that remind her of the African presence on the island.[10] Navigating the tension between her parents' divergent fusings of history and identity, Clare becomes diaspora conscious and revises Du Bois's concept of double consciousness. However, instead of a Du Boisian split or doubled consciousness, we find a schizophrenic Clare Savage. Because Clare's biological genealogy is complicated by the social/class rules of life in Jamaica, she must conflate her father's simple understanding of identity as rooted in color and her mother's location of selfhood in place.

Clare recognizes color privilege and its subsequent unfairness and cruelty. Though she attended school on a scholarship, she is treated quite differently from and by the dark-skinned scholarship girls. Though this may seem to allow a space for Clare to seek refuge in her ignorance, she acknowledges that she herself appreciated her looks, for "[s]he lived in a world where the worst thing to be—especially if you were a girl—was to be dark. The only thing worse was to be dead" (*Abeng* 77). The degree to which Clare really understood her luck is tested in her childhood friendship with Zoe.

To create a bank from which Clare could withdraw memories of home and kin, Kitty "makes" Clare spend her summers working on her grandmother's land. Clare's understanding of the privileges she carries, not only through color but also because her grandmother is a landowner, takes concrete shape during these visits. In fact, it is the latter privilege that "gives" her a friendship with Zoe. Miss Ruthie, Zoe's mother, "squats" with her daughters on Miss Mattie's land, and the summer that both girls are ten, "Miss Mattie sent to Breeze Hill to ask Miss Ruthie whether Zoe could be her granddaughter's playmate. Zoe was at the front steps the next morning" (*Abeng* 93). The girls are intimidated by the presence of the other, Clare afraid Zoe will resent being requested, and Zoe suspicious that Clare, a "town girl and fair enough to be taken as buckra," would look down on her. Soon, however, they become comfortable with each other, and their friendship takes shape (*Abeng* 94). While "the shadow of color permeated" all relationships at her school in Kingston, in St. Elizabeth with Zoe, Clare can leave that behind (*Abeng* 100).

When Clare refuses to allow Zoe to try on her bathing suit, "they stumble across" their difference and a confrontation ensues (*Abeng* 100). Just as Clare had relied on her grandmother's instructions to Miss Ruthie to secure her playmate, so too had Miss Mattie instructed Clare that the newer bathing suit was hers. She tells Zoe: "A no fe me to decide. Grandma e'en told me" (101). Zoe, only wanting to try on the suit, not use it for swimming, responded that Clare is "one wuthless cuffy, passing off [herself] as buckra." Angered, Clare strikes Zoe and they fight until Clare begs for peace and agrees that she is indeed "one true cuffy and stingy as one dog" (*Abeng* 101).

Zoe's invocation of the language of class and color crystallizes how the fight is about more than the bathing suit. By naming Clare a "cuffy"—an "upstart," one who fancies herself upper class—and asserting that Clare is passing as "buckra"—a white person, specifically one representing the ruling class—she focuses on Clare's unwitting assertion of her economic status and social power. Zoe emphasizes that although the bond between color and class may at times seem invisible, its power is inescapable. Her contextualization of her dispute with Clare in class terms is reinforced later when, after being excluded from a game by some boys, Clare devises a plan for her and Zoe to hunt a wild pig in the bush of her grandmother's property. Zoe resists Clare's plan initially but eventually goes along with her friend. Zoe's resistance is related to Clare's distance from the immediacy of the outcome. Clare will leave for Kingston, but Zoe would have to hear the "talk and [she] would have fe tek on all de contention" (*Abeng* 117).

When the incident turns disastrous and Clare accidentally shoots her grandmother's bull, Zoe scolds Clare and explains their different social positions:

> Wunna is town gal, and wunna papa is buckra. Wunna talk buckra. . . . Dis place no matter a wunna a-tall, a-tall. Dis here is fe me territory. Kingston is fe wunna. Me will be here all me life—me will be market woman like fe me mama. Me will have fe beg land fe me pickney to live pon. Wunna will go a England, den maybe America to university, and when we meet later we will be different smaddy. But we is different smaddy now. (*Abeng* 118)

Zoe confounds Clare with her pronouncements on difference, and Clare struggles to convince Zoe that they are the same, of the same land. Yet she knows that she is different and the same. Zoe defines the divide between them in terms of land and property, "territory," highlighting as well the class distinction inherent in their color difference. Most importantly, this exchange underscores the relationship between place and identity. The way that color and class are read in Jamaica complicates the relationship between diaspora sisters within this geographic territory. Clare and Zoe's relationship becomes an interior representation of the difficulty inherent in establishing more global kinship ties.

Cliff more explicitly engages diaspora cross-cultural connections through a distant cousin on her father's side, Robert, who had brought a man home from Montego Bay. While the family's response to the "dearest friend" (*Abeng* 124) was characterized by homophobic suspicion, this was not the most explicitly articulated point of contention. The friend was a black American, and "didn't [Robert] know that American Negroes were very different from Jamaicans" (125). Furthermore, "the dearest friend was dark— Dark American Negroes were not our kind of people a-tall a-tall" (*Abeng* 125). This distinction of color outside of the national borders of Jamaica is especially relevant, given that Creoleness necessitates the acceptance of conflicting forms of experience and history, and of differing definitions of the self.

When Cliff talks about "claiming an identity" she was taught to despise, she articulates an attempt not only to comprehend the simultaneity of the various facets of her self in shaping her identity *but also* an attempt to link her experiences with those of others to whom she and her protagonist are bound.[11] Through Zoe and Clare's relationship and the sidebar about Robert, Cliff exposes how local identity concerns can shape global relations. In this way, the memory of Robert provides a backdrop against which Clare can make sense of these ideas about color and class privilege. For Clare, as for Cliff, this understanding would involve the place of other African descendants in her life, space, and sense of herself.

This inquiry returns us to Cliff's poem "The Laughing Mulatto," where the narrator recalls the three sisters, each of whom, with their notes and desire for secrecy, sought agency and subjectivity at the foot of their silent "idol." They recognize her as a slate of passive objectivity upon which Black peoples were written. Similarly, Clare attempted to use her relationship with Zoe, to in fact use Zoe, as a slate onto which she could inscribe a diaspora identity and thus unite the conflict of being both a Freeman and Savage. Clare fashions a mythical narrative of her friendship with Zoe: "Secrecy was something they held between themselves" (94), never discussing their difference.

In conversation with Walker and the myths that constrict Tashi, Cliff's Clare relies on a myth that requires that Zoe must not only passively comply, but also not acknowledge her awareness of Clare's desire. She must be, like the statue, a silent structure, and like Tashi a conformist to tradition. However, as Cliff's poem suggests, when such mobile subjects "speak" or attempt to participate in their meaning-making, they are not heard, just as Clare could not hear Zoe's exhortation or allow her to resist the pig hunt. These silenced voices manifest the scars of a colonized subjectivity, not just a taking over of the body, but a claiming of the body's right to affirm itself and tell its stories. Like Walker, Clare must come to understand not only the damage that color and class privilege has caused in her own life, but also how she has used that privilege to affect events in others' lives, as well. The result is a diaspora consciousness, the capacity to see oneself through and as both "other" and "self." Ancestral history and positionality manifest Clare's schizophrenia and Tashi's double-consciousness and the effects of relocation on their state.

Class Revolution: For the Creole, Is There No Telephone to Heaven?

No Telephone to Heaven also concerns the migration of Clare and her family to America, a place the family "knew about mainly from the movies shown in Kingston" (54). As the mythology of America dictates, Boy Savage saw his family's move as a new beginning; Kitty Savage, in contrast, sees it as a dangerous venture. In Jamaica the Savages are members of the dominant class, due in part to Boy's English lineage and landownership by Kitty's family. The confidence that each has in their position is shaken when the family arrives in Miami. Emphasizing his commitment to invisibility, Boy travels the "secondary roads" from Miami to New York. Their trip marks Kitty's and Boy's sharply contrasting styles of adapting to their new country. While the former ignores the racist slogans pervading their travel through Georgia, Kitty quickly realizes how unwelcome they are in the land of immigrants: "No Statue of Liberty for them—oh, no—their emblem of welcome . . . was a small sign. . . . A MAN WAS LYNCHED YESTERDAY, it said. 'Hello, America,' Kitty muttered to herself" (54). The Savages' class in Jamaica had no bearing on the shifting subject position they would occupy in America. As if there were any doubts, repeated assaults on people of color serve as vivid reminders: "RACIAL SELF-RESPECT IS NOT BIGOTRY, black ink on a white background promised, as if explaining the sign post beside it: YOU ARE IN KLAN COUNTRY" (58). The construction of these texts, the white background with black ink, reifies the potential for Clare's black body to be inscribed with references that her father would bid her reject but her mother cannot escape, for in America bigotry will, if allowed, erode her self-respect.[12] Although the Savages are largely the objects of racist slurs in America, they have themselves participated in discrimination.

The Savages separate themselves not only from the maids who serve them, but also from the black Americans with whom they share more than a slave history. Once the Savages reach New York, Kitty is made aware that though black Americans "were [their] shipmates, as surely as the slaves who crossed the Middle Passage together," she should make no attempt to identify with them. They are instructed, in no uncertain terms, to "Pass if you can. . . . This is not a country for us" (61). Her cousin Winston informs the family that "the Black people here are not from us. The white people here are not from us" (61).[13] Despite the similarity in skin shade, Winston highlights a distinction between American Negroes and Jamaican blacks. Though he is dark-skinned, the black American woman with whom he works still sees him as different.

Boy Savage takes a job driving a truck for White's Sanitary Laundry, and Kitty takes on clerical work in the office of the same company. The clerical work is minuscule, so Kitty is given the task of sending "'helpful hints' to the laundry customers" (72). In a manner that heeds Boy's advice to remain invisible, and Winston's to "pass if you can," Kitty takes on the persona of "Mrs. White, the imaginary wife of an imaginary man" (73). The laundry hints are messages premade and inserted into the finished laundry. They have an accompanying image of "an older woman with gentle gray curls, pink skin . . . clear blue eyes. Slender sculpted nose ending well above her smooth top lip" (74). Kitty becomes Mrs. White by virtue of her responsibility for placing the messages into the laundry. Kitty finds this a heinous task, for Mrs. White represented a "powerless icon masked as mother" (80). This characterization epitomizes Kitty's experience of her own reality, both generally in her life with Boy and particularly in America. Separated from her home and barred from replicating its pleasures (e.g., securing and preparing the food she likes), Kitty grows impetuous and takes on feelings of displacement characteristic of exiles.

Mrs. White becomes the focus of her rage against the discourses that imprison her, primarily those of American conceptions of race. Where "silence" had once been "Kitty's finest weapon" (*Abeng* 131), surreptitious voice now becomes a more viable option. She supplants the notes provided for her with ones she herself creates:

> Her pen traced balloons . . . putting words in Mrs. White's pert mouth.
>
> WE CAN CLEAN YOUR CLOTHES BUT NOT YOUR HEART. AMERI-CA IS CRUEL. CONSIDER KINDNESS FOR A CHANGE.
> WHITE PEOPLE CAN BE BLACK-HEARTED. THE LIFE YOU LIVE WILL BE VISITED ON YOUR CHILDREN.
> MARCUS GARVEY WAS RIGHT. (81)

Boy discovers the writings and is outraged; however, Kitty goes undetected by Mr. B. until she writes the final note, menacing and threatening: "HELLO. MRS. WHITE IS DEAD. MY NAME IS MRS. BLACK. I KILLED HER"; Kitty feels "free and released," believing she has erased the narratives that constrict her (83).

Critical to my discussion of blackwomen's diaspora relations, Kitty sits between two darker-skinned American black women as she sends her "hints," yet there is no interaction amongst them. In fact, their relationship makes Winston's earlier suggestion to "pass if you can" all the more compelling: "Kitty and the women in the packing room—named Georgia and Virginia—spoke only from necessity. But when Kitty was in the outer office . . . she could hear them chatting softly, laughing" (77). Kitty is excluded by these women because she is not of them, for being lighter skinned and a Jamaican black entitles her to a difference that her coworkers resent and mistrust. In this place, shared history and diaspora membership do not elide difference. Kitty is offended by their exclusion of her, for their names return her to the journey to New York and the back roads where American hatred and racism made her their target. When Kitty returns to work after sending the last note, she discovers that a patron brought in a picture of Mrs. Black along "with instructions to discontinue serving as their laundry" (83). Before Kitty can confess, she is told that Georgia and Virginia have been fired because "that kind is no good. Unstable" (270).

The controlling metaphors of racist discourse are in material reality obscured. Kitty unwittingly subscribes to them while attempting to undermine them. The contraband notes she writes to the white clients are offered to counter the association between black and evil. Yet when she institutes Mrs. Black, Kitty reinforces the white ideology that developed Mrs. White.

The illusion of her race is broken with the last note, and even after she confesses, she is not believed. Mr. B. replies, "a nice girl like you? Don't be crazy . . . No, I can't believe that" (84). For her "luxury" two black women have been cast into potential poverty. Kitty rebels against the privilege she has simultaneously enjoyed and castigated, and she resigns from the laundry.

This textual moment again recalls the "three sisters" gathered at the feet of "the laughing mulatto" statue who left "notes" exacting "promises" never told. Kitty could not sustain the promise of her note—to kill (what had created) Mrs. White—for she was unable to remove her mask, to recognize that, in effect, she had become Mrs. White, or to penetrate the surface of her "sisters." Like Walker, Kitty cannot escape the consciousness she developed in her home place. Cliff articulates, in "If I Could Write This in Fire," a position that parallels Kitty's here.

Cliff explains that "it was never a question of passing," yet Kitty resigned herself to having others, mostly Boy, construct a self within which she would exist in America (*Land of Look Behind* 71). Yet, at the time "when their visions got out of hand," she would "startle them with a flash of anger." In America, Kitty has a "life lived within [herself]. A life cut off" from all that she knows and understands of herself. Through the guise of Mrs. White, Kitty "hid from [her] real sources," and her guise also reveals how much her real sources were "hidden" from her (71). Just as Clare presents the camouflage of Americanness in her war with America, so too does Kitty hide behind the guise of Mrs. White to rage against the oppressive racist discourses threatening her. Both of their resistance struggles follow scripts controlled by the very powers they wish to resist and thus are doomed to failure (King 44). Kitty leaves America, taking her younger daughter Jenny and leaving Clare with her father.

In the novel, and in Clare's life, Kitty functions as the axis for representing Creole struggles toward diaspora consciousness: "Kitty encircled a subject which became taboo between father and daughter," and when Kitty dies, Clare comes to understand this axis, and how it is the center for her own life (*No Telephone to Heaven* 102). Kitty leaves America to return to her rightful place, a space where she had become herself. America serves as a temporary place for Clare on her own journey to becoming, her journey back to Jamaica. Clare begins the paradoxical duality of identity with the conflicting ties to her parents. Her development is marked by the struggle between her identification with a class-conscious light-skinned father and a silent, strong mother's love for her homeland.

Boy Savage adamantly chastises Clare: "You are too much like your mother for your own good. . . . You are an American now. You need to know what that means" (*No Telephone* 102). Boy attempts to instruct Clare in a necessary redefinition of herself in relation to her new place, her new home. Survival in an environment hostile to one's being requires camouflage, a complex matrix of masking and passing. Hence, Clare Savage, a signifying duality, rejects both of her parental homes and flees to London to begin "her life alone" (109).

As with her mother in America, the racism Clare faces in England comes in the form of signs: "white bedsheet with black paint," announcing "KAFFIRS! NIGGERS! WOGS! PAKIS! GET OUT! KEEP BRITAIN WHITE!" (*No Telephone* 137) The privilege of color passed on to her by her father allows her to be recipient of a schoolmate's confidence that "nig-nogs are a witty lot" (137), to which the rage she inherited from her mother endows her to direct the classmate to "go fuck yourself!" (138). London proves for Clare what America proved for Kitty—that there is no place like home. So Clare, armed to educate the young Jamaicans in the genuine archaeology of their history, returns to Jamaica. Her homecoming, though intended to be rehabilitative and restorative, is marred with difficulty stemming from migration and isolation, for Clare "was educated in several tongues, the mastery of which should have kept her from that truck [No Telephone to Heaven] and stifled her longing to know Coromantee" (106). Yet the conditions of her color and class privilege compel her to embrace the thing that is muted within her, to remove one mask and find her self.[14]

Perhaps Barbara Lalla is right in her assertion that guilt of [her] privilege (184, 187) characterizes Clare Savage's narrative presence, but I would suggest that she is caught in some form of the proverbial cultural limbo. Clare and Boy Savage are not yet English, although such an identity is commensurate with their education and training. Yet, they are in some measure unwilling to participate in the vitality of island folk culture.[15]

Separated from her mother and father, Clare makes her final quest for her self and her place. In *Abeng* the narrator comments on the separation of families and how the anxieties induced by this disconnectedness and isolation affect individual development, *becoming*. Furthermore, the narrator explains how these effects have been internalized and suffered by the islanders "unto themselves"; realizing that there was "no telephone to heaven," the islanders reason that the "cause of their losses lay in themselves—their people's *wuthlessness*" (17).

The connections associated with destroyed families become a metaphor, as

Paul Gilroy suggests, for the separation of blacks from their African heritage. Here, colonialism, with its erasure of the colonized's historical memory, becomes synonymous with a system that separates families and erases memories of kin. Later, the narrator provides an exact connection between this sense of *wuthlessness* and the islanders' ignorance about their African past: "They did not know about the Kingdom of the Ashanti or the Kingdom of the Dahomey, where most of their ancestors had come from. They did not imagine that Black Africans had commanded thousands of warriors. Built universities. Created systems of law. Devised languages. Wrote history. Poetry. Were traders. Artists. Diplomats" (*Abeng* 20). This is the history "bleached from [their] minds" (*Land of Look Behind* 14) While the life of a Creole is not romanticized, and neither is there an idealization of the erased past, Cliff does outline the painful limitations of Creole identity and the ambiguous adjustments that Creoles must endure. Clare's wuthlessness is manifest in her schizophrenia.

Cliff's prosaic-poetic collection *The Land of Look Behind* makes this split consciousness subtly clear. The title of the collection recalls Jamaica's colonial past, refers to its geographical present, and speaks to its progress toward the future. The colonial past is invoked in the narratives themselves, but Cliff's piece also shares its title with an earlier account of travel to Jamaica by a British subject. W. J. Brown, M.P., published his *The Land of Look Behind* in 1949.[16] In the introduction he explains that "a title is a name, and there is magic in names . . . to name a thing . . . is to affect it" (v). Here, the "member of Parliament" uses *affect* in the context of influence or change. While this is appropriate, Cliff uses the same title to affect or simulate the history of the reference as a metaphor for the experiences of her protagonists. According to Brown, "In Jamaica there is part of the interior, up in the hills, which has a peculiar history of its own. In the days of slavery, slaves who had committed some offence, or who rebelled against ill-treatment by capricious and sometimes brutal masters, would sometimes flee into these hills, and there hide from their pursuers . . ." (xiii). This community developed, and its inhabitants became autonomous and established their own laws. These people were led by a Brown, and the writer W. J. Brown, claims this leader as an ancestor and implies a link between him and Jamaica. Names, in this context, associate people with places and histories with identities. Cliff revisits this political intersection of Britishness and Jamaicanness, and from this mix emerges her Creole protagonist.

While Alice Walker can "search her mother's gardens" and excavate a tradition that sustains her and allows her to sow seeds connecting her to the past and projecting her into the future of womanists, Cliff's gardening "is a pitched battle against" her mother and her sister and is "thus contaminated" (*Land of Look Behind* 49). The notion of contamination illuminates the history of Cliff's diaspora position, how she is named diaspora kin, yet that kinship is tainted by her status as Creole, defying morphological race identification. The dilemma of the Creole is not whether to connect to the histories of her sisters, but rather the delicacy of how that connection can be forged against conflicting class positions of color privilege. Cliff demonstrates that Du Bois's intellectual vision belongs to and speaks to Caribbean women of African descent as well. Yet she manifests an extension of that vision that redefines the parameters of the diaspora, erasing the monolithic unity that race family suggests. For Cliff, the African diaspora family is bound by history and experience, though her color and class may exclude her from its invocation of blackness.

chapter four

"Blackwomen Always Seem to Be Going Through *Changes*": Ama Ata Aidoo Voices a History Muted[1]

The history of place is critical to any inquiry into the African diaspora, as it is the center of the cultural matrix formed by the intersection of ethnicity, class, and gender. Walker works to (re)construct the body (corporal and corporeal) of the sistered kinship, only intimating how location defines the sisters. Michelle Cliff identifies the complex social dimensions of place that inform identity and make the establishment and maintenance of kinship ties difficult. In her narratives, Ama Ata Aidoo identifies the inextricable connection between African women's and African diaspora women's condition and the whole condition of Africa. As a Ghanaian, Aidoo's literary focus extends from her social vision. She explains that "there are things relating to our world, as African people, which are . . . throbbing" and immediate (James 15). One "throbbing" issue to which she has devoted attention is the silenced history regarding why and how Africans came to be displaced and dispersed across the globe. She recalls that "go[ing] to places where there are concentrations of other black peoples" aided her resolution to "face the question," in her literature and by other means available to her, to explain just why "so many [African peoples] are in Harlem and so many in the West Indies" (Vincent 35).

Both her travels and the fact that Aidoo constructs her inquiry from Ghana make place especially central to any discussion of her work. As the homeland of choice for W. E. B. Du Bois and the nation led to independence by Du Bois's student Kwame Nkrumah, Ghana holds a particular significance for African Americans making the trek back home.[2] Acknowledging this historical relationship and hearing its whispers, all of Aidoo's fiction and plays allude to diasporic relations, and her characters encourage an open conversation.

Aidoo's plays, more explicitly than her fiction and poetry, manifest her diaspora consciousness, examining the relationships between members of the African race family. As well, drama allows Aidoo to simulate dialogues across historical time and space in ways that prose cannot. Through drama and theater, Aidoo crystallizes the heteroglossia that defines literature and must define any notion of diaspora kinship. Literary texts, like any other kind of utterance, depend not only on the activity of their authors,[3] but also on the sociohistorical forces in effect when the text is produced and consumed. Particularly, Pan Africanism and "double consciousness" frame the conversations that Aidoo initiates between continental Africans and their kin abroad. Her plays are utterances that speak to *why Africans sold their brothers to the whites.* Like all utterances, Aidoo's dramas are cemented in a cultural matrix from which they can never be fully extricated.

Aidoo's *Dilemma of a Ghost* and *Anowa* help us to understand this web of influences and the consequences for diaspora kinship. The issues highlighted by the presence of Eulalie, the African American protagonist in *Dilemma,* in Africa strongly relate to Alice Walker's readings of African women. Especially, Aidoo highlights how a search for kin, like Walker's and Eulalie's, can lead to unwitting participation in the proliferation of stereotypes and misconceptions about the other women, and even to silencing them. Aidoo does not directly engage the Caribbean in her texts, nor does Alice Walker, and this absence amplifies the dislocation that Clare Savage, Cliff's protagonist, feels. Cliff's narratives focus on the dilemma of the Creole, the identity that is both and neither. Not only is she a silent Creole, but inquiries into the diaspora have geographically silenced her, as well. Though these specific issues are not explored in depth in *Changes,* the main character Esi's experiences emphasize the importance of dialogue to any kinship relationship.

Aidoo's work takes the politics of the diaspora relationship and "throw[s] the floor open to debate"; she demonstrates that "the function of [her] story-telling is to initiate" (Abrahams 16–17). *Changes* (re)initiates issues raised in Aidoo's previous work. For example, the novel interrogates constructions of Aidoo's place as homeland within other diasporic cultural fictions.[4] Dispelling myths about the African ur-mother, Aidoo crafts diverse Ghanaian women and examines their struggles to locate themselves in their postcolonial world. As well, she makes clear how the history of colonialism makes locating the ur-African—geographical, cultural, and biological—mother or sister difficult, thereby allowing us to understand Cliff's struggle and read the personal quest underlying Walker's.

Shared Oppression, Separate Spaces: Aidoo's Terms of Kinship

Aidoo's diaspora consciousness and her desire for a grounded sistered kinship direct us to *Anowa,* her second play, where Aidoo briefly tells the tale of the

slave trade and the dissemination of Africans across the globe. The text itself
is dialogic, and its voices speak to the various intricacies of the institution of
slavery—the manufacturing of the diaspora. The text instigates conversations
amongst the readers, all the while conducting an exploratory discussion of its
own. The characters talk around the subject they wish the readers to directly
engage.

We are introduced to the eponymous Anowa as "a child of several incarna-
tions," a returned spirit of a formerly dead child (*Anowa* 7). In her analysis of
"diasporic ruptures" in Aidoo's drama, Maureen Eke terms these characterizations as evidencing Anowa's status as "abiku," or "a wandered child who
returns again and again from the dead to plague its mother" (62). Such a
haunting characterizes Aidoo's conception of diasporic history. For Aidoo, facing the question of how the diaspora came to be is critical, "because [she
thinks] it is part of what is eating us up. You can't cover up history" (Vincent
35). By setting the play in the late nineteenth century, approximately 1870,
Aidoo immediately opens the Pandora's box that contains the grievous history
of slavery both within and without Africa.[5]

Anowa is a beautiful woman who rejects societal authority to marry Kofi
Ako, a man she herself has chosen. They gain wealth in trading, but soon
Kofi expands their trading to include human cargo. Anowa refuses any of the
benefits from her husband's business in stocking and selling slaves, for she
finds "something unwholesome about making slaves of men" (39). A pivotal
moment in the play comes when Anowa reveals her dream that she, like
Africa, gave birth to the men and women who were captured into slavery:

> I dreamt that I was a big, big woman. And from my insides were huge holes out
> of which poured men, women and children. And the sea was boiling hot and
> steaming. And as it boiled, it threw many, many giant lobsters, boiled lobsters,
> each of whom as it fell turned into a man or woman, but keeping its lobster head
> and claws. And they rushed to where I sat and seized the men and women as
> they poured out of me, and they tore them apart, and dashed them to the
> ground and stamped upon them. (46)

Anowa's dream critiques the history that it recounts, as it is "imbued
with metaphors of power, conquest and domination" (Eke 67). Just as Kitty,
in *No Telephone to Heaven,* turns over her daughter Clare to the European-
identified Boy, this dream "conflates Anowa with slavery and 'mother Africa'"
as well as reclaims "the maternal as a site of dispossession and rupture"
(Davies 1994, 76). Anowa, as mother, manifests the notion of diaspora sis-

tered kinship that grounds my work. Indeed, she confesses her nightmare, and "the women of the house told me not to mention the dream again" (107). This instruction silences the medium, but it also constructs a deafness in the potential receivers of the message—things that should be left unspoken, even when uttered, are not heard.

In furtherance of the Atlantic slave trade, children are taken from the figurative wombs of their mothers, and like Anowa they grow up with many questions they are forbidden to ask. In *Anowa*, Aidoo engages the homelessness that haunts Clare Savage and the cultural dilemma that confounds Tashi. These characters' conditions are metaphorically presented as mother lack. The dream's manifest metaphors of captivity and restriction capsulize the diaspora orphanage created by slavery.

The play also reveals that women are the particular keepers of this horror, as Anowa recounts to the reader a story told to her by her grandmother, Nana, about her travels to lands far away from Africa. In this place across a "sea that is bigger than any river and boils without being hot," Nana sees "houses whose foundations are wider than the biggest roads" in Africa (44). These houses were built large, she tells Anowa, to house the slaves—"[those] who are bought and sold" (45). Anowa asks Nana if African men sold their brothers, sisters, and children to the whites, and Nana not only replies that she does not know, but informs Anowa that "no one talks of these things anymore," for presumably "they have forgotten" (46).

Aidoo demonstrates that all has not been forgotten. Though the dream is horrific, it symbolizes an entry into the past, a passage to understanding her present. For Aidoo, the dream breaks a historical silence, a rebellious act equaling the songs rendered by the bare-bottomed baby girls in *Possessing the Secret of Joy*. Like Clare in *No Telephone to Heaven* and *Abeng*, Anowa struggles with the history of her homeland and attempts to navigate the constraints that accompany her membership in her family. The boiling sea is the source of Anowa's historical memory.

Anowa's dream makes the sea a "site of memory." Toni Morrison, in an article titled "The Site of Memory," explains that "all water has a perfect memory and is forever trying to get back to where it was. Writers are like that, remembering where we were . . . and forever trying to get back to where it was" (305). Morrison's memory allows her to create out of the various cultural texts she has read a spiritual and mythic fiction of Africa. The middle passage is the water source into which she wades. African Americans are constantly diving for the sunken treasure of their past; it is the "hyphen" of their existence. However, Aidoo, with this play, initiates Africans' wading into that source and responds to sociohistorical prohibitions against it. The historical inquiry necessary for a developing diaspora consciousness requires movement; leave-taking, from the shore to the sea of memory, is central.

Aidoo's play ends with Anowa leaving home. Her mother warns her, "I am waiting for you to come back with your rags and nakedness" (17), yet Anowa is already naked, stripped to the bare realities of history. Hence, she can leave her home, assured: "I shall walk so well that I will not find my feet back here again" (19). Like Clare Savage, Anowa sets out on a perpetual search for home. While Clare is buried into the ground of Jamaica, literally making her body the land, we are left with the legacy of Anowa's inquiry. Anowa's quest, having named herself a wayfarer with "no home, no family, no village" (36), allegorizes the diaspora child's orphanage and her trek to cure her homelessness.

Focusing on the marriage between Ghanaian Ato Yawson and an African American woman, Eulalie Rush, Aidoo's first play, *Dilemma of a Ghost,* deals with this orphanage and speaks to the question of whether or not the diasporic child is in fact African, and if so, to what degree.[6] The history *Anowa* provides frames the dilemma of this play. Within this context, the play directs the reader to the specific gendered dynamics within the diaspora kinship system. While the "ghost" of the title refers to a ghost from children's folklore, lingering at the junction between two slave trading posts and pondering to which city it should go, I read it as a metaphor for silent history. Refusing to specify Cape Coast or Elmina, the ghost repeats, "I don't know, I can't tell" (*Dilemma of a Ghost* 28). Critical readings thus far have indicated that the dilemma is Ato's, and he is haunted by his inability to decide which way he should go: toward the West, symbolized by his wife, or toward tradition, embodied by his family.

The ghost's obvious indecision not withstanding, I read the presence as the spirit of the bodies kept in the posts, who "lived in a mute territory; dead to feeling and protest. . . . the legions, sold by sisters, stolen by brothers, bought by strangers, enslaved by the greedy and betrayed by history" (Angelou 98). The ghost appears to Ato because he has unknowingly invoked the ghost of diaspora history, and he has given shape to the muted memories in the being of Eulalie. Her presence, however, manifests the complexity of return and awakens the dilemma of how Africans are to deal with their past. I contend that what Ato lacks is a diaspora consciousness, and his silence is due to Africans' own lack of knowledge about their historical implication in the slave trade.

As well, Eulalie's conflicting emotions toward Africa represent the African American end of the dilemma. Her expectations are akin to those described by Alex Haley in *Roots*. In the final chapter of that journal of his ancestry, Haley describes Juffure, the village of his ancestry, thus: "like most back-country villages, it was still very much as it was two hundred years ago" (576). Like most idealized descriptions, this one is unrealistic, but its purpose is to provide an element of identity. Aidoo casts her prodigal daughter's return with similar notions of hyperbolized paradise. Eulalie tells Ato that she will relax among the "palm trees, the azure sea, the sun and golden beaches" (36). She describes Africa in terms of storybook myths, and, as Ato tells her, "a tourist brochure" (36). More directly, she speaks to her dead mother's spirit and tells her, "I've come to the very source. I've come to Africa and I hope that where'er you are, you sort of know and approve" (19).[7]

This return invokes the pragmatic reality of African American treks to Ghana. In fact, many African Americans embarked on "the return" and searched for "an authentic expression of their 'African roots'" (Walters 103). Maya Angelou records her return, but unlike that of Alex Haley, her Africa is not Edenic. In *All God's Children Need Travelling Shoes,* she discusses her trek to Ghana in 1962, and she demonstrates the familiar strangeness that incapacitates both Eulalie and Ato. She explains: "I doubted if I, or any Black from the diaspora, could return to Africa. We wore skeletons of old despair like necklaces, heralding our arrival, and we were branded with cynicism" (76). Angelou is ever conscious of the differences between black Americans and Africans, but she is also conscious of her historical links to Africa. Like Angelou, Eulalie ventured to Africa in search of a home; Eulalie marries Ato hoping to address her double consciousness and reconcile the two parts of herself. However, instead of existing, like Angelou, as a native stranger in Ato's land, Eulalie yearns to be simply native, to annihilate her strangeness; she thinks for once she is going to be at home.

Though Eulalie's desire was to find peace and harmony in her new marriage, in her new home with her new family, their ignorance of each other brings only chaos and suspicion. When Ato informs his family that he will marry an American, they fear that she is white. Attempting to assuage his family's inquiry about Eulalie's lineage—to whom does she belong—Ato relies thoroughly on the theory of the race family, clarifying that despite geography, his wife "is as black as we all are" (17). To his mind, the articulation of this racialized reality is enough, though he gives no thought to how the difference in geographical location manifests cultural and social divergences that make negotiation with marital and racial kinship necessary.

Upon hearing that Eulalie is black but belongs to no tribe, Nana, Ato's grandmother, responds, "[s]ince I was born, I have not heard of a human being born out of the womb of a woman who has no tribe. Are there trees which never have any roots?" (11). Ato explains that Eulalie's family was amongst the Africans taken to America as slaves, awakening the sleeping history.

The routes of displacement have demanded a replanting of roots, and this (re)rooting cannot be eschewed, for as Eddy Harris learned on his own travel through Africa, the African American "is another race, newborn and distinct, forged in the blast furnace of slavery, tempered and tested in the foundry of survival. . . . Yes, Africa is the birthplace of mankind. Africa is the land of my ancestor. But, Africa is not home" (28–29, 312). Though Ato takes comfort in the fact that Eulalie's "ancestors were of [their] ancestors," his mother and grandmother are pulled up short by the history of slavery and the pragmatic difficulty of integrating into their lived reality a body that bears a history nobody speaks of anymore (*Anowa* 46).

In fact, Nana ponders how she can incorporate her new daughter into their family story—what she will tell the ancestors about "[t]he daughter of slaves who came from the white man's land" (14). The importance of their familial narrative outweighs their obligations to the prodigal daughter (Eke 74). Just as Walker does not know from what tribe she descends, so too is Eulalie still a stranger, for Aidoo makes clear the impracticality of the diaspora daughter's return: "For they often do not know the names of the founders of their houses" (*Anowa* 92). As well, though, Aidoo makes clear that the corrective for this potentially eternal exile lies with both the sojourner and those who inhabit the land to which she returns, for if her clan has forgotten or refuses to claim her, their familial narratives are disrupted. Unless the silence is challenged, the practical consequence for Africa and her children is an equally numb "nightmare of dismembering parturition" (Johnson 112). Not only does the orphan mourn, but the mother also mourns her lost children.

Aidoo investigates the consequences of elided conversations and the mutual lack of knowledge between Ghanaians and black Americans in her first novel, *Our Sister Killjoy,* as well.[8] Sissie's love letter, the epistolary final chapter of the novel, voices her concerns over violations of Africa by non-Africans and Africans alike. Like the ghastly history that Anowa is forbidden to speak of and that Eulalie conjures, so too is the glorious history of Africa silenced, for Sissie "cannot give voice to her soul and still have her heard" (112). The mandates for language—which language and what can be produced in language—create a situation where "the messengers of [Sissie's] mind always come shackled" (*Our Sister Killjoy* 112). Recalling the chains that contained her diaspora kin, Sissie parallels the colonial imposition of European languages with the banning of certain utterances. Like Anowa, Sissie speaks the unspoken and distinguishes internal slavery from the Atlantic slave trade. She explains that though they "were never able to discuss some of these matters related to our group survival" (114), witnessing the behavior of her fellow Africans abroad, their dogged pursuit of Western materialism at the expense of their obligations at home, she understands that this is how the diaspora came to be.

Among these matters is the "old story" and a "painful one" about how intoxication from the lure of wealth and profit led Africans to sell their kin. Sissie places "a curse on those who for money would ruin the earth and trade in human miseries" (115). Sissie's love letter functions to similarly invoke the history unearthed in the earlier plays and to parallel the experiences of Africans and their diaspora relatives. Particularly, Sissie acknowledges that Africans were made slaves and exploited as free labor "with the help of the gun and some of our own relatives" (114). Undoubtedly, Sissie speaks of the forced labor and exploitation under colonialism as well as internal slavery, but these painful stories are not untold. However, as evidenced by Anowa and her "dream" and the ghost at the junction, the complicity of Africans in what came to be known as the Atlantic slave trade *is* an old, painful, and untold story.

Sissie charges that the ruthless expansion of Western civilization "chokes all life and even eliminates whole races of people in its path" (112). As a result, diaspora children are in search of a home place within a history that marks them as orphans, and Aidoo parallels this orphanage as a way to manifest her diaspora consciousness. She recognizes that the sense of orphanage is shared by continental Africans who, like Nana, are also alienated from their continuing historical narrative. In exile herself, Sissie recognizes that Africans themselves participate in this genocide. The "love letter" demonstrates that Aidoo's gaze is definitely inward, because the love it professes is both private/personal and public/political.

Moreover, *Changes* offers us an opportunity to examine that inward gaze and how it is directed from without. It is a gaze directed in part by assumptions such as those of African Americans like Eulalie. *Changes* is a novel about African women, but its representations of these women result from the narrative willingness to engage the Other's gaze and to turn what the Other sees on its head. Like *Possessing the Secret of Joy, Changes* is a cultural fiction. It is a novel about gendered culture in Africa, and how it has been inscribed, described, and transcribed from the outside. But, like *No Telephone to Heaven* and *Abeng,* it is about how one woman's attempt to make her place within the context of her sociopolitical world results in her unexpected role as a revolutionary. This call to revolution is a manifest sign of diaspora consciousness. In what appears to be the individual desire to understand self and place, and to navigate spaces, diaspora-conscious women are compelled to tackle larger issues of communal survival. Here, Aidoo mirrors Cliff's reformation of *littérature engagée,* literature that engages the political and cultural issues at stake during its production.

In *Changes,* Ama Ata Aidoo tackles Paul Rabinow's challenge that we "anthropologize the West" and examine its perceived universals for their "historical peculiarities" (241). This anthropologizing is what Cliff attempts as she interrogates the American film crew's desire to *narrate* Nanny's life. Alice Walker's awareness of the historically peculiar relationship between Africa and the West does not prevent her from organizing Tashi's world around the bodily sexual politics of patriarchy. With *Changes,* Aidoo suggests that such categorizing is sometimes inappropriate. A text is a border phenomenon; it takes place between speakers—readers and writers—and is embedded in social factors. It exists on the border of the tradition(s) that produce it and the larger tradition(s) within which its producer and consumer exist. Hence, we must explore not only the large body of the texts, but also the grammars of discourse that delimit and constitute cultural experience: the sites of our cultural memory. Diaspora women's bodies become texts situated at crossroads between present home places and past sites of memory and history. Through *Changes,* Aidoo shows the link between cultural body and text, as she reconfigures the ur-sister as a site of memory.

Esi Sekyi, an Africa(n) Woman, or Complexities of Gender in Place

Changes is the story of Esi Sekyi, and on the surface, the novel focuses on Esi's experiences in search of love on acceptable terms. However, it is also a novel about traditions of loving: love of partner, love of friend, love of family, love of nation. In the story of Esi we find several traditions intersecting, being made and remade. First, Aidoo engages the representations of African women already out there in the critical discourse and the Western peculiarities projected onto them. In addition, she manipulates these characterizations as she questions the stories that have been, can be, should be, and/or/but may never be told. As well, the novel is a text of representational struggle and revision, a restructuring of traditional modes of organization, yielding not only a "(re)new(ed) structure, but a new lens through which to view the preexisting one(s)" (Holloway 13). In this text Aidoo revises two modes of organizing African women's experience, and as such she reinstitutes the African woman into the sistered kinship.

While Cliff struggles to articulate a Creole position within the kinship, Aidoo revises the version of African women that grounds Walker's Tashi and even informs Cliff's Nanny. Each of these women embodies one of the seven primary stereotypes of African women: "[t]he Earthmother, concubine, door-mat of a wife, the sacrificial lamb, the high life floozy, the 'been-to,' and the willing mechanism in a polygamous drama" (Bell 491). While these con-structions are in many ways the consequence of waning diaspora memory and the desire to idolize the mother/land, voices from the continent have partici-pated in this typecasting, as well. Aidoo writes against two major scripts. First, in traditional African male-authored texts, these archetypes allowed for monolithic characterizations of African women's experiences, fixing the women, regardless of class, within the prevailing stereotypes. In fact, one of the leading male African writers, Nigeria's Chinua Achebe, says that such rep-resentations have functioned to create and reinforce "all kinds of myths that support the suppression of the [African] woman" (4). He further states that the time has come for this to change and that "the woman herself will be in the forefront in designing what her new role is going to be" (4). Second, the dominance of male representations allowed Western, mostly white, middle-class feminists to theorize and discourse on African women through sexual liberationist politics, creating a script of their own. In fact, Aidoo tells us that some of these feminists have gone so far as to declare that women like her are "bourgeois African women [who] are in no position to speak for ordinary African women in the village" ("'That Capacious Topic'" 153).

Ama Ata Aidoo's women-centered stories become problematic when taken alongside Western and African male "narratives of gender" (de Lauretis 25). Critical colloquies like that of Achebe and some Western feminists provoked interest in African women's fiction.[9] This concentrated critical inquiry evi-denced the dearth of attention previously paid to female novelists and opened a dialogue with African women on (1) Africa; (2) women's experiences in Africa; (3) the place of women in Africa; and (4) men's representation of women in their writing. However, the central foci of these critical discus-sions were feminism, interrogations of male readings, or both—thus, de-emphasizing African women while conversing about them. For example, instead of discussing the politics of the literary work, critics challenged the degree to which African women were feminist. Many critics, like Molara Ogundipe-Leslie, lamented that "many African female writers like to declare that they are not feminists, as if it were a crime to be a feminist" (11). It is my sense that the politics of feminism are not objectionable to these writers, but the discourse engendered by use(s) of that particular term is what they find unacceptable.

Aidoo stated that she would not "protest" if critics and readers of her work choose to call her "feminist," but she intimates that she is not a feminist sole-ly *because* she writes about women ("Unwelcome Pals" 40). For Aidoo, being a feminist is more than demonstrating a sincere regard for women and writ-ing about women's experiences. Buchi Emecheta rejected the politico-cultur-al location of feminist discourse and the term "feminism" itself: "I will not be called a feminist *here* because it is European. It is as simple as that. I just resent that. Otherwise, if you look at everything I do, it's what feminists do too; but it is just that [the term] comes from Europe, or European women, and I don't like being defined by them" (Grandquist and Stotesbury 19). These two writers would argue that not every woman who makes a political statement assessing and/or critiquing the social position of women is a femi-nist. Most importantly, Aidoo and Emecheta link gender and location; they see the discourse of feminism as located outside of where they and their sub-jects experience gender.

Changes illustrates how Aidoo works within and against discourses of Western feminist and male-constructed monoliths of African women's expe-riences. As Walker's womanism guides her fiction, Aidoo's version of a femi-nist writer informs hers. Aidoo's particular aim is to force us to question past representations of African women, to challenge our presumptions and assumptions about the African woman's condition, and in so doing to (re)write a discourse of feminism that treats an African woman on her own grounds.

Aidoo as a writing subject consciously writes through her multiplicity and against foreign and domestic essentialist transcriptions of her identity. She constructs subjects who serve to subvert, diffuse, and/or dislocate dominant forms of social discourse (Butler 1990, 141–43; Nfah-Abbenyi 283). Aidoo writes as a diaspora-conscious nationalist/womanist, and as such she creates women who confront their realities, laboring not only to survive as individ-ual gendered subjects, but also as contributing members of a society strug-gling to revolutionize itself. This dual commitment has been defined by Frank and others as "the African woman's bind," "the African woman's dilem-ma," and, borrowing from Buchi Emecheta's novel, "the double yoke" (Umeh 178). However, *Changes* clarifies that duality is not a *bind,* nor are the often conflicting requirements of these existences a *dilemma* that must be resolved.

Instead, the dual task of purpose is the woman's social consciousness, her life, the goal toward which, in frustration sometimes and even in anguish, she steadily labors.

Aidoo directly engages this presumption of an *intrinsic* choice that African women must make between social and financial independence on the one hand and Africanness on the other. When the novel opens, we are first introduced to Esi as a professional woman—"from the Department of Urban Statistics"—then as a wife and mother (4). Immediately, the novel forces us to confront the "paramount question that nearly all [African novels by women] ask . . . how can the contemporary African woman negotiate her way between the claims of tradition and modernization, how can she be rendered whole again?" (Frank 18). Particularly, the bind is connected to the social institutions—such as family, community, economy—with which women choose to associate. In the same moment, Aidoo addresses the important reality of female sexual presence in male-authored African fiction, women as appendages or tools in the hands of someone male (Davies and Graves, *Ngambika* v; Frank 16).

First, while radical feminists argue that "sexual freedom requires sexual equality of partners and their equal respect for one another as both subjects and body," libertarian feminists suggest that "sexual freedom requires oppositional practices, that is, transgressing socially respectable categories of sexuality and refusing to draw the line on what counts as politically correct sexuality" (A. Ferguson 108–9). The African woman's bind, then, reflects repressive social categories of sexuality that preclude "equal respect" for women as subjects and bodies. Aidoo addresses these issues through another examination of language.

Early in the novel, Esi is trying to come to terms with her feelings about what she describes as a "marital rape" and imagines herself presenting a paper entitled "The Prevalence of Marital Rape in the Urban African Environment" (10). Her presentation, she imagines, receives "boos from the men, and uncomfortable titters from the women" (11). At this moment, Aidoo engages the issues of language raised by Sissie. With her body, Esi tells a new story, one breaking through to its "own meaning and its own expression across an environment full of alien words" and alien constructs (Bakhtin 277). Though the narrator later asserts that "the society could not possible [*sic*] have an indigenous word for [marital rape]" because "sex is something a man claims from his wife as his right" (12–13), we are still left with Esi's struggle to name her experience, and the force that naming has for her sense of herself as an individual and social being. Esi's struggle parallels that of the orphan to name her family. Both evidence the "magic power of the word," language as "a creative act" (Jahn, *Muntu* 121, 133). Janheinz Jahn explains that an object "is 'complete' only when it is Nommo, a productive word, effective word or function" (172). Thus, an image, experiential or corporeal, has no intrinsic meaning until it is named. Because language encodes our experiences and places us within certain frames of reality and experience, the orphan must locate a space for herself within the space of family, just as Esi must find the vehicle for relaying her experience in the language of her people.

Directly, Esi's reflections reveal that neither we nor Esi can demonstrate that her language "never" had a word for marital rape. Such reductionist conclusions are problematic, for so much of Africa has been transplanted elsewhere and claimed by others as their own. For example, in Aidoo's poem "Mardi Gras," from the collection *Someone Talking to Sometime,* the issue of food as a means of erasing African signs appears. New Orleans symbolically becomes Little Africa, USA, and the narrator responds with equal fury to Esi when she realizes that even when Africa is obviously visible, people still refuse to acknowledge her. Most notably, the foods that most reveal Africa's presence, like "gumbo," are assigned to the French and Spanish.[10] In contrast to this practice, Esi's characterization of that sex act with her husband as "marital rape" conjures a self-representation of the colonial body, an expression of its scars from history. Aidoo turns this silenced African history on its head as Esi, unlike Tashi, claims her body as her own, and is unwilling to compromise or trade off on that ownership or allow anyone else to write its narrative.[11]

Issues of language collectively cohere Aidoo's two novels into the diaspora project initiated by her plays. *Our Sister Killjoy* aims to loosen the ease with which Africans move further and further away from their history. The first chapter title, "Into a Bad Dream," not only speaks the novel's aim "to dispense with any Western parameters" (Holloway 148), but it also redirects readers to *Anowa* and casts Sissie's sojourn as parallel to the diaspora orphan's. Sissie becomes a colonized child—whose mind, like Clare Savage's, has been bleached—trapped by the languages and voices of her history. Readers cannot help but recall Eulalie's dislocation and isolation. Yet, instead of doing away with time, distance, and place as Holloway suggests (148), Sissie reinvokes the legacy of these three. She forces the reader, diaspora and nondiaspora alike, to understand that in our codes of naming we recall the "precious something" lost in the boiling sea, whose voice has been lulled by the "hopes, fears and fantasies" that give diaspora cultural fictions the tone of "frustrated speech" (Holloway 60).

After the incident of marital rape, Esi leaves Oko and begins a relationship with Ali Kondey. Ali is a womanizer who reveres and admires his father, and he consequently tries hard to emulate him, professionally—as a trade sales-man—and personally—as a philanderer (24). Significantly, though, the arena of sexual politics is "the only way in which Ali was not like his father" (24). Whereas "Ali's father preferred his women young and tender [who] had to be virgins of course" (23), "Ali liked his women mature, and he had no special use for virginity" (24), rejecting the idea forged by Alice Walker that African men desire virgins, women whose sexuality has been regulated and restrained for the increased sexual pleasure of men.[12]

Indeed, Ali's attitude toward women convinces Esi that he would respect her in ways Oko did not and could not. Appropriately, through his thoughts we are allowed to confront the social forces of tradition that confound African women. After recognizing, and admiring, the ease with which Esi shares her nakedness with him, Ali reflects upon the narratives of victimization that are foisted upon African women: "traditional shyness and contempt for the biology of women; Islamic suppressive ideas about women; English Victorian prudery and French hypocrisy" (75). These discourses posit the woman as merely a passive object, and internalization and re-articulations of them ignore the degree to which sexuality and understandings of sexuality can be simultaneously oppressive and liberating—an arena for political struggle. Indeed, Esi's ease with her body suggests that the relationship between the individual and the social forces that Ali describes is probably not one of total social determination nor of socialization. To the contrary, Esi demonstrates that socialization is an ongoing theoretical endeavor never fully realized in practice. One is never fully socialized, but is always in the process of socialization. Hence, Esi emerges not as a victim of colonialism and/or patriarchy, but instead a dynamic woman, and a significant dynamic in her life is polygamy.

At the same moment that Esi has freed herself from her strangulating marriage to Oko, she enters a polygamous marriage. Because her "society [does] not admit that single women to exist," Esi decides that she will remarry and become Ali Kondey's second wife (*Changes* 47). This polygamous relationship provides a vital commentary on the issue of changes. It also epitomizes the diversity within diaspora kinship. After agreeing that they will marry and that Esi will become Ali's second wife, Ali presents Esi with a ring and Esi questions Ali about its implications, inciting a discussion of the differences between polygamy and bigamy, and highlighting the sistered kinship. Esi explains that "Fusena already wears your ring" (89–90). Invoking Fusena dissects kinship and the ways in which polygamy is liberating for Esi but restrictive of Fusena's rights as first wife. Fusena is an almost creole presence in her silence and absence from the text, yet Esi invites her by criticizing her exclusion.

Ali does not follow traditional custom, which would allow Fusena to choose and approve his choice of a second wife. Instead, he chooses and does not consult her at all. Furthermore, Esi initially abides this effacing of Fusena's voice. Like Walker's allowing her womanist mission to silence Tashi and erase African women's subjectivity, Aidoo exposes how Esi's desires for free expression of her sexuality and accommodating companionship could potentially isolate Fusena. Not only has Ali's masculinist politic rendered theirs a nonegalitarian relationship, encouraging Fusena to give up a level of equality along with her educational pursuits, but also Esi's liberatory drives further disempower Fusena by eroding her dominion in the compartmentalized space of wife.[13] Esi recognizes that in the polygamous marriage the second wife is never to undermine the power and status of the first wife, and she recognizes that wearing Ali's ring would do just that to Fusena's station as "Mrs. Ali Kondey" (90). Nonetheless, she does not act on that recognition and as such alienates herself from one of her sisters, and she laments that rupture.[14]

This familial triangle brings me back to the global kinship conceived through the Atlantic slave trade. Esi here becomes a metaphor for the ways in which African Americans, citizens of the most powerful country in the world, have for so long dictated and written the rules of diaspora relations, using the history of their place, cultural and geographical, as the only intellectual point of departure, silencing the Creole and eclipsing the African.

Changes presents Esi's speaking voices and the different voices that she confronts. These confronted voices represent the varied possibilities for African women. Esi is presented as a woman not willing to sit and wait for things to happen. She makes things happen. Esi changes, goes through changes, is put through changes, and changes things. The other two major female characters in the novel—Fusena Kondey and Opokuya Dakwa—are affected by changes. Accordingly, this novel presents a variety of ways that gender can be experienced in Africa. In the same way that Michelle Cliff complicates the notion of the "race family" model of diaspora kinship by exploring the intersections between "race" and color and class in Jamaica, so too does Aidoo concentrate her inquiry into diaspora kinship in the politics of her place. *Changes* recognizes that polygamy is a central issue in African women's struggle to identify with their sisters across the sea. Just as Alice Walker called upon Zora Neale Hurston and the literary heritage of African American women, Ama Ata Aidoo's *Changes* revisits and revises readings of Mariama Bâ's representation of polygamy in *So Long a Letter.*

Sisterhood and Individual Freedom: Fusena Kondey, the Other Woman

Using Mariama Bâ's *So Long a Letter,* Aidoo demonstrates the delicate balance that diaspora women must strike if they are to be simultaneously engaged in a struggle against oppression and a sisterhood that sustains their individual freedoms. Bâ offers two characters, Aïssatou and Ramatoulaye, who embody different directions followed by women. The epistolary style allows the reader to eavesdrop on Ramatoulaye's account of her life; she speaks but not directly to us. We hear the intimate details of Ramatoulaye's life as revealed through her thoughts, feelings, and desires, all of which are shared with a friend, a secret utterance.

bell hooks tells us that "within feminist circles, silence is often seen as the sexist 'right speech of womanhood'—the sign of woman's repression," but non-WASP women, hooks suggests, have never been *that* silent (*Talking Back* 6). Though the latter group of women's voices may have been ignored, they spoke and often disguised their speech so that the tendency to "tune it out" would be lessened. It is my position that *Changes* talks back to *So Long a Letter,* just as both women writers talk back to their society. Under the guise of revelatory private thoughts and personal correspondence, these authors have constructed women "with sharp tongues" who would not deny themselves the "right to voice, to authorship" (*Talking Back* 6). Significantly, though, while Bâ's protagonist views herself as a victim and moves from silence to speech, Esi is always an agent, speaking herself and seeking to further exercise her agency. In *Changes,* Bâ's colonized body—African (and) woman—speaks, utters its injury, and negates its assigned muted condition. However, Ramatoulaye uses the holy requirement, *mirasse,* to expose not only Moudou's finances, but also his personal secrets. Ramatoulaye writes what she could not speak. It is on this point that I see Esi as a revision of Ramatoulaye. Esi indeed invokes traditions indigenous to her people, but her acts of subversion and challenge are loudly spoken. Esi has "made speech [her] birthright" (*Talking Back* 6).

Furthermore, Aidoo revises Ramatoulaye by offering us Fusena Kondey and Esi Sekyi. These two women assume postures represented by the divided consciousness that Ramatoulaye presents in her letter. Aidoo splits

Ramatoulaye and develops two different women from Bâ's shell of a woman, emphasizing the bond between women and our responsibilities to each other. At the novel's end, Ramatoulaye tells Aïssatou, her best friend: "I warn you already, I have not given up wanting to refashion my life. Despite everything—disappointments and humiliation—hope still lives within me. It is from the dirty and nauseating humus that the green plant sprouts into life, and I can feel new buds springing up in me" (89). We never know what becomes of Ramatoulaye in her struggle to "refashion" herself. However, Aidoo not only offers us a look into the choices available to women like these two, but she also allows us to witness the consequences of the choices they make.

Both of the women in Bâ's novel are confronted with the news that their husbands have taken second wives without first consulting them. Aïssatou is livid when she hears the news that her Mawdo Bâ has married again, and she writes him a scathing letter before leaving him. She makes a new life for herself as an interpreter in New York, declaring to her husband, her friend, and her society that "[p]rinces master their feelings to fulfil their duties. 'Others' bend their hands, and, in silence, accept a destiny that oppresses them. That, briefly put, is the internal ordering of our society, with its absurd divisions. I will not yield to it" (31). In similar fashion, while Esi suggests that marital rape may not have existed prior to her experience, she manages to find a course of action that not only serves her best interests, but also puts Oko, and vicariously other men, on notice that such deeds by husbands toward their wives are neither acceptable nor tolerable.

Unlike Esi, Aïssatou rejects her society's values when she decides that her society's support of Mawdo's behavior is unacceptable and pursues her determined course of action; she decides to abandon him and that society. In contrast, Esi does not ever consider leaving her world; she is determined to live within her society while negotiating a space there for people like her, women like her. Aïssatou has no such conviction. Clearly, for Bâ, just as Western women may have the legal right and social "freedom" to reject polygamous behavior from their husbands, African women also have that option. However, for diaspora-conscious women, for whom orphanage is a major issue, there is the revolutionary choice: to remain amongst your kin. For those who choose to function and exist within a society that sanctions and recognizes polygamy, there are other choices available to them. Aidoo demonstrates some of these choices.

Silence is one such choice, the one Ramatoulaye and Fusena elect, although even in their silences they give voice to very different possibilities.

The signifyin(g) on Bâ's text is most clear when we look at Ramatoulaye's and Fusena's responses to marriage and their roles as wife. Marriage for both of these women offers a comfort that they value more than "independence," and each of them recognizes the trade-offs they have made. But only Fusena analyzes the consequences of this trade-off: that of being only a wife. Ramatoulaye accepts her station as a wife and concentrates on developing that aspect of her life. She maintains a home and works outside, but her largest commitment is to her home and her husband. Fusena, on the other hand, chooses balance, dividing herself equally and faithfully to both of her two jobs: "When she was in the kiosk, she was there. And of course when she was at home, she was home" (99).

In *Changes,* Fusena has fashioned a life for herself that is equal to her life as wife, and for that Ali respects her. Hence, when she discovers that her husband plans to take a second wife, she is angry not about the traditions he ignores, but that her co-wife "has a university degree" (99). Fusena is reminded of the time Ali persuaded her not to continue her education and tried to convince her that idleness was a wife's privilege. Luckily, she had reasoned that Ali's "wealth or ability to support her was a matter only of mild importance—just something that would make [her] life easier," and pursued selling in the marketplace (67). Significantly, Ramatoulaye, like Esi, has a university degree. She was "among the first pioneers of the promotion of African women" (Bâ 14). If it could be argued that she rejects polygamy because Western education has lifted her "out of the bog of traditional superstition and custom" (Bâ 15), then it could also be convincingly argued that this education equally had no effect on Esi's decision to willingly enter into such a marriage. Thus, the influence and power of Western education is predicated upon how the subject locates herself in her society and positions herself vis-à-vis its operating discourses.

The notable divergence between Ramatoulaye's position and Fusena's has to do with how each defines herself and her choices. The former chooses to stay with her husband as a wife and maintain her home, while the latter pursues interests outside her marriage. Ramatoulaye and Fusena both choose the instability of dependence, because their other choice, "liberation," as Ramatoulaye calls it, is too difficult. Ramatoulaye is dedicated to her society's notions of the sanctity of the family. She is "persuaded" of the necessary "complementarity of man and woman" (88). Further, she sees the "success of a nation" (93) as dependent on the success of the couple and the family they develop. Rewriting this nationalist narrative, Aidoo exposes how adherence to such beliefs allows men to oppress women, for while women adhere to the rules, men do not. Traditionally, the decision to expand the family through a second or third marriage involves the couple; both partners must agree that the second marriage will not disrupt the home they are in the process of forming. But, in both cases, Ali's and Moudou's, the first wife was not involved in either the decision to take a co-wife or the selection of an appropriate woman.

Aidoo challenges the silencing of woman's power in this domain. Ramatoulaye is silent when she is informed of her husband's new marriage; her feelings are neither solicited nor volunteered. Likewise, Fusena is silent when the women in her village try to convince her that Ali's taking another wife is not the worst thing for their marriage. But Aidoo highlights how their silence is affected by the choices their sisters made as well as the behavior of their husbands.

That Ramatoulaye and Fusena become unstable within the security of the family is chiefly the result of the modern African man's bind and Esi's lack of a sense of sistered kinship. As Esi tells us, there is much "insolence [in the person of] the modern African man" (91). Fusena has a home with Ali but recognizes that a woman with more education may take that away. Esi does not recognize her participation in Fusena's silencing until Fusena's voice is all but gone.

The pivotal issue is not so much contempt for polygamy but confusion about Fusena's place in this whole affair, and who should invite her voice and give her a space from which to speak. The power of sistered kinship comes with Fusena and Esi's reasonings that "[i]t was a man's world [and] you only survived if you knew how to live in it as a woman" (107). For Fusena, living as a woman means being a wife and a mother, and being silent about your pain. But it also means having something else, like her kiosk. For Esi, living as a woman is having what you want, including someone who respects you for wanting. By offering the contrasting models of women's roles, Aidoo contests Walker's implication that Tashi's choices are either to live always under the repression of patriarchy or to renounce her affiliation with the Olinkans. Walker sees the only freedom as that which comes from totally destroying the social systems that repress. Aidoo confesses that some women are confined to certain realities; there are some colonial bodies whose stories will never be rewritten.

However, there are others who write. While M'Lissa and Tashi have no choices, Esi and Fusena do, and they live the consequences of those choices. Walker is right to suggest that "resistance is the secret of joy" (*Possessing* 281), but there are various resistances: the *one* she valorizes and the *others* she ignores. It is through not resisting limits that Ramatoulaye and Fusena allow for instable dependence. This notion of an instable dependence characterizes the relationship that Cliff's Clare Savage manages with her history. Cliff does not allow Clare a stable history, for the Creole's life is fashioned against the embattled legacy of color/race and class privilege. Moreover, Aidoo forces women to come to terms with the correlation between their individual choices and their sister's consequences, and this reinforces her sense of feminism as a totalizing and revolutionary pragmatic.

There is no resolution to *Changes,* for there is no simple and/or uncomplicated answer to the question it attempts to answer. I believe that Aidoo's point is just that. The status of diaspora women's kinship is an issue that is yet to be resolved, as is the status of all women regardless of origin. Esi's story is not finished, for the silences of history have not yet been voiced for some colonial bodies. African women—all women—are some of those bodies. Aidoo offers a reading of African women that confirms Diana Fuss's assertion that identity is "historically contingent and constantly subject to change and redefinition" (20). Identity is a story told, retold, revised, and unwritten. Aidoo finds that the image of Africa is equal to the fictional reality she makes, especially the reality of our connection.

Aidoo tells us she "write[s] about things that people will feel uncomfortable about," things she hopes people will squint at (James 15). As I read *Anowa, Dilemma of a Ghost, Our Sister Killjoy,* and *Changes,* I do indeed squint. As I read her works, I am drawn to her female subjects, and as a black woman, I am drawn to identify with their pains and pleasures. Yet, through my squint, I begin to see the limits of such empathy, based in large part on my own search for diaspora sistered kinship. Indeed, the construction of reality in Aidoo's fiction challenges any blackwoman-centered reading, while at once speaking *to* that diaspora consciousness. Because Aidoo explores issues of gender, a sociocultural and political construct, the squint is an adequate description of the approximate shared vision between Aidoo, Walker, Cliff, and myself. Certainly Aidoo is concerned about African women and her diaspora sisters; however, she is equally concerned about how the first of these is represented by the others. Because of the varying ways in which womanness is constructed and experienced within different social systems, reading gendered behaviors across cultures can be a tricky business. *Changes* is a novel that questions the facility with which readings like those in *Possessing* are constructed. *Abeng* calls our attention to the need to unravel our histories and fashion them anew through a revolutionary project. Taken collectively, all three novels acknowledge that there is *No Telephone to Heaven,* no quick avenue through the complex matrices of geography, class, and color that the history of African dispersal has made.

five

ite it in. . . . Put the sex right up on in there!": Walker, Cliff, and Aidoo Sexualize and (Re)Map the Diaspora

Female homosociality presents itself as a relative stranger in discourses on diaspora blackwomen's lives, receiving passages, notes, and mere mentions in most critical studies. This absence is socially and intellectually profound, so much so that as I write, I struggle with trappings of convention in language, thought, and politic. I use the term *female homosociality* to make a distinction between women loving women outside of active sexual relationships and women who are sexually active with women. As such, I use female homosociality in the former sense and lesbian in the latter. The former identifies women who love men and resist patriarchy, all the while able to simultaneously exist within heterosexual contracts, or they may be women who conscientiously object to marriage. While these women have not been sexually involved with women, they have a passionate commitment to women.

I invoke Adrienne Rich's notion of the lesbian continuum, which she defines as including "a range—through each woman's life and throughout history—of woman's identified experience; not that a woman has had or consciously desired genital sexual experience from another woman" (23). However, Rich claims that such a "lesbian existence" requires the "rejection of a compulsory way of life. It is also a direct or indirect attack on male right of access to women," making it an outright sociopolitical identity (23–24). Though I reject the strictness of this definition, I embrace the notion of integrating female friendships and comradeship into the erotic zone constructed by conflations of lesbianism and female homosociality (Rich 24). Thus, we can construct a continuum of relations that include adolescent and adult friendships, sexual relations between women, and the cohabitation of single, divorced, widowed, aged women—lesbian or not. Given the criticism of *The Color Purple*'s failure to construct for Celie a fully subversive sexuality

(Hoogland, for example), I agree with Cora Kaplan's suggestion that such readings limit the potential of a lesbian continuum, and "any pleasure that accrues to women who take part in heterosexual acts is therefore necessarily tainted; at the extreme of this position women who 'go with men' are considered collaborators" (52). Though I limit lesbian love to acts of sex, and recognize this as a problematic and perhaps volatile limiting, I see this configuration as the line of female relationships represented in the texts I examine here.

There are several levels at which sexuality evinces itself in the writings of Walker, Cliff, and Aidoo. Most obviously, these women writers all engage, on some level, female homosexuality, and with this line of inquiry the three women's texts intersect. As I have identified earlier, Walker's narratives are steadily crafted quilts of blackwomen's bodies, and such fabricking does not overlook the ways in which those bodies act; sex is one of these significant actings.

Judith Butler suggests that "'sex' is, thus, not simply what one has, or a static description of what one is: it will be one of the norms by which one becomes viable at all, that qualifies a body for life" (*Bodies That Matter* 2). Blackwomen's bodies, physically and practically, become territory open to development of a black nation, and therefore they become property of men. Aidoo makes this clear in *Changes* where Esi and Opokuya discuss the former's leaving her husband. Opokuya explains that marriage is the central stage upon which women play their societal roles, reminding Esi that theirs was a society that "had no patience with the unmarried woman." Indeed "her single state was an insult to the glorious manhood of [their] men" (48).

In each of the novels I discuss here, the relationship between woman and man is dissected through inversion and invocation of the first human connection in life, the bond between mother and child. Erasing, or turning into, a man is a recurrent theme for these three writers, highlighting their inversion of the homosocial order that privileges male contracts. Additionally, Walker and Cliff invert the male-designed progression of female sexual desire away from the mother. Though Walker and Aidoo invoke this situatedness, they invoke it to challenge it. Celie and Esi follow in a tradition of their creators' women who live with or leave their husbands and live alone, successfully. Some of these women have children and some do not, but all live on their own terms and offer alternative versions to traditional heterosexual relationships in the process. Moreover, through their narratives, Walker, Aidoo, and Cliff posit that not only are women without men a diaspora reality, but so are female homosociality and lesbianism. None of these prevents nation building, but instead each allows blackwomen to contribute in ways beyond reproduction of new male warriors. In this way and for these women, "writin' is fightin.'"[1] In fact, the battle begins with women claiming their own bodies. Walker claims that Tashi's body is devalued for its sexed femaleness, and Aidoo highlights prescriptive sexual roles and sexual performances that embody the ways that life is hard on women (*Changes* 51).

Demonstrating the idea of blackwomen's bodies as male territory, I recall my earlier discussion of the mummy woman—from Walker's *Meridian*—Marilene O'Shay, the circus attraction who, in life a white woman, in death becomes darker and lies in her rigid form as testimony of what happens to women who allow themselves to be "corrupted by the honey-tongue of evil-doers" (20). We find O'Shay's sister in Cliff's "Burning Bush." In the latter story from Cliff's *Bodies of Water,* we see the patchwork woman, "the girl from Martinique," presenting herself as a circus attraction, using her body as a canvas protesting her biraciality (76). She whitewashes herself, and "a piece of cloth wrapped her breasts and wound itself behind her, crossing her body beneath the navel," exposing her stomach, the center of her body, her womb, which is also "patches of black bumped against ivory" (76). The narratives' notions of whitewash reflect the conscious erasure and/or camouflage of black female homosocial and lesbian presences. The workings of such camouflage are made clear by Aidoo's commentary on the perceptions of women without men. Not only do "societies [refuse to admit that] single women exist" (Aidoo, *Changes* 48), but, as Collins notes, "despite the fact that some of the most prominent and powerful Black women thinkers . . . were and are lesbians, this precept often remains unacknowledged" or is, in fact, whitewashed (Collins 65).[2]

In this chapter, I interrupt that logic through an acknowledgment of the black female homosocial presence in blackwomen's diaspora literature and examine the various manifestations of that presence. While Aidoo constructs a narrative that engages lesbianism exclusively, Walker and Cliff interrogate female homosexuality and question the boundaries of sex/gender themselves. Dialogue between Cliff's *Abeng* and *No Telephone to Heaven,* Walker's *The Color Purple* and *By the Light of My Father's Smile,* and Aidoo's *Our Sister Killjoy* reveals a struggle with the politics of female homosociality aligned with struggles of diaspora subjectivity. The body becomes the place where these three writers intersect most compellingly. In turn, female homosexuality becomes an aspect of identity rescued from the void by the diaspora conscious, accenting this gendered and sexual bond between women as a compulsory aspect of diaspora studies.

The Sacred Places of Sisterly Convers(at)ions

In all of the novels studied here, the women present their initial sexual choices as having been made for them. Celie discovers her love for Shug only after realizing that her forced relationship with Mr. is unfulfilling. It is through Shug's teaching that Celie discovers that she loves Shug as women are supposed to love men. The prescribed roles of men and women in human relations also shadow Clare's relationship with Zoe and Sissie's with Marija. Hence, these novels reveal the ways in which Others have directed diaspora women's sexuality and manifest the ends of such direction for the women themselves.

Walker's *The Color Purple* offers a representation of female homosocial development that is at once lesbian and not exclusively so. As well, the novel's representations of Celie's sexual life create an intersection between narratives of female homosexuality and the narratives of kinship that introduce both this book and this chapter. Seeing the novel from what she "provisionally" calls "a lesbian perspective," Renée Hoogland sees such a convergence as "neutralizing," a perversion of the "potentially subversive force" of Celie's lesbian sexuality (12, 21).[3] To the contrary, I see the melding of lesbian love "into love of kin" (Hoogland 21) as a strength in the novel's overall representation of a diaspora politic.

The novel begins with the primary love relationship between women, that of mother and daughter, but this too is disrupted. Showing the damage of compulsory heterosexuality, the novel opens with Celie's mother too exhausted from, and even made physically ill by, the demands of reproduction. The absence of this space for establishing the father's maleness propels him to force Celie "to do what [her] mammy wouldn't," or more appropriately could not (11). This mother absence is significant in all the narratives under discussion here. Mother absence figuratively represents diaspora women's alienness, as the lesbian woman becomes an orphan, an exile. Indeed, Celie's life with Mr. confirms her state of exile prior to Shug Avery's arrival, and the novel also reveals her orphanage, in that her mother has died, and her father is not her biological father. In performing as/for her mother, Celie bears two children, but she is left physically barren by the rapes and births. Not only does she lose her own mother, but she is also no longer able to participate in the fullness of the heterosexual contract, which requires women to reproduce and mother children, thereby erasing her mark as a woman.[4]

To extract himself from Celie, Pa explains that, to the good fortune of Mr., who has too many children already, Celie cannot bear any children: "God done fixed her" (18). In a final blow, he names Celie male, for her greatest attribute is that "she can work like a man" (18). Celie, then, becomes a lady, for "*woman* [means], well, someone capable of breeding. It [is] strictly a biological term and, because [the notion of black women as breeders is] associated with slavery, [it is] considered derogatory" (Walker, *Temple* 171).[5] Ironically, accepting her inscription as a lady, Mr. agrees to take Celie, along with the cow that is her dowry.

Early in the novel, Walker shapes her womanist praxis and the nexus of the novel: a concern for the wholeness of communities, both women and men. She posits that compulsory heterosexuality and its social and physical demands destroy both men and women. Not only is Celie's mother destroyed by reproductive demands, but also Celie is reduced to invisibility by her forced sexual encounters with Mr., who uses her for nothing but work and sex; when she is not engaged in either of these activities, he brutalizes her physically. Drawing the connection between womanist praxis and theory herself, Walker highlights that "it is a mistake to assume that Celie's meekness makes her saint and Mister's brutality makes him a devil. The point is, neither of these people is healthy. They are, in fact, dreadfully ill and they manifest their disease according to culturally derived sex roles" (*Living by the Word* 80).

When Celie first sees a picture of Shug Avery, which falls out of Mr.'s wallet when he comes to beg for Nettie's hand, she instantly recognizes her as beautiful, and her attraction to Shug is born. During the painful sex acts with Mr., Celie sustains herself, is comforted and able to embrace her husband, by thinking of Shug Avery and knowing that "what he doing to [her] he done to Shug Avery and maybe she like it" (21). When she encounters the corporeal Shug Avery, and bathes her body—a body that Mr. shuns outside of sex—she amorously writes, "First time I got full sight of Shug Avery long black body with it black plum nipples, look like her mouth, I thought I had turned into a man" (53). Reinvoking her father's frame, but shifting the context, Celie's homoerotic desires expose her reliance on heterosexual order, an order that while making sense to her mind, does not explain her body. When Shug comes and stays with them, and eventually solicits Celie's feelings about the former's relationship with her husband, Celie seizes the opportunity to gain insight into heterosexual workings. Celie describes the clinical reality that is her and Mr.'s sexual life and her dislike of the "business" of it (*The Color Purple* 79). Her description highlights the contractual nature of heterosexual arrangements. Through her confession of distaste, Celie discovers that despite Mr.'s disciplining her to the contrary, her emotional/physical/sexual feelings are important. Shug simultaneously confesses her pleasure at sex with Mr. and legitimates Celie's experience, making it make sense to Celie's mind and body. In an act that grounds their homosocial contract, Shug tells Celie that she is still a virgin, restoring to Celie the purity that Pa stole through word and deed and endowing her with a power over her own body.

That these conversations are spoken privately between the two women, that their relationship receives no *out*side acknowledgment or commentary, highlights a problem within the novel and the diaspora's formulations of a muted homophobia. That Celie and Shug's relationship is private, defined by quiet moments and secret conversations between the two of them alone, invokes Collins's criticism of a wider approach to black lesbianism. hooks argues that homophobia is denied, or at least idealistically ignored, in the novel. In the face of such critique, however, Shug and Celie's confessions become quite telling. Lesbian sexuality as well as overindulged heterosexuality are things one has to confess—either a passion for or a passionate distaste of. This reference undergirds the power of Walker's representation. By the novel's conclusion, there is no space for phobias of any kind, and no need for confessions. Hence, a novel that began as Celie's confessions to God, her telling of the secret sins that are her life, ends with a reshaped and accepting God, who makes nothing dirty and is pleased when we love, cherish, and embrace the things he has made, whatever and however we do so. Revising God breaks the homosocial contract between men, and Celie learns to see God not as one of them—male—but as everywhere, and everyone, embracing all differences; lesbian love grows to be normal, in the eyes of a reenvisioned God.

Erasing the notion of sexuality as a sinful and dirty thing, Shug encourages Celie to look at herself "down there," to see herself. Celie complies bashfully and is excited by the vision of her own vagina, parting the lips to expose "a wet rose" (79).[6] Shug instructs her as to the location of her clitoris, and just as she finds, touches it, and stimulates herself, Shug notices that the men are returning. Hurrying to dress herself for male eyes, Celie says, "I feel like us been doing something wrong" (80). Indeed, they have. Celie, with Shug's help, has traveled outside the boundaries of compulsory heterosexuality; the two of them have removed the whitewash. Just as Mr.'s exclusion from the bond between her and Nettie so threatened him that he sent Nettie away, here, as well, Celie is forming a forbidden homosocial contract. In a contrasting response, Mr. and Celie are able to share Shug and recognize and validate each other's love for her, and to be changed by both that love and their mutual acceptance of the different ways they love her.

The entrancing of Shug into the privacy of Celie's sexuality emphasizes Mr.'s inability to further control Celie. The making of Shug as male, in Mr.'s mind, allows him to come to terms with the damage that compulsory heterosexuality has done to him, which is necessary for womanist healing to take place. Celie overcomes her affliction, as well; where she earlier read Shug's comment that Sofia "look like a good time" as indicating how "Shug talk and act sometimes like a man," by the novel's closing she is able to recognize the range of women's being (82).

This closeness frees Celie from Albert, although Shug invites heterosexual contracts. While a reading of this binding as a weakness in the novel's lesbian articulation is legitimate, I read it as placing female homosexual desire on a continuum of women's ways of loving. Loving a woman does not exclude loving a man, sexually or not. Demonstratively, when Shug returns from Memphis with her newly acquired husband, Grady, Celie is tempted to hate him, but her love for Shug is stronger than her feeling of betrayal. And, while their husbands are out drinking, the two women lie in bed together. Here, Celie utters the secret she was only to tell God, how her father raped her and fathered her two children. While Fruola argues that this utterance breaks the authority of men (638–41), I suggest that it is not as much about undermining male authority as it is about establishing the sanctity of female homosocial desire. Celie feels love, sees God in Shug, and begins to equate their compassion with Godly love. As Shug kisses the tears that fall from Celie's eyes, the latter admits her aloneness, orphanage, and exile: "Mama die, I tell Shug, My sister Nettie run away. Mr. come get me to take care dese rotten children. He never ast me nothing bout myself . . . nobody ever love me" (109). With an utterance paralleling the matrimonial "I do," Shug affirms Celie with a declaration of love; like virgins in the nuptial chamber, they each announce their ignorance about lesbian lovemaking, then proceed to feel their way, to make love to and with each other.

The notion of women's love as synchronous and inseparable from kinship love is a central axis for integrating narratives of lesbian love into diaspora discourses. Diaspora consciousness, as I have constructed it, recognizes the significance of differences but struggles to negotiate a space where these differences do not matter in terms of status or privilege. Walker herself acknowledges that as a child growing up in Eatonton, Georgia, she has no memory "of ever seeing, hearing about, or even being able to imagine homosexuality"; furthermore, even in a friendship with a woman who had many lovers, their conversations never included her lesbian relationships (*Living* 163–64). The silence of black homosexuals and their place as particularly *out*side—outside community life, outside the realm of conversation—is what Walker mutes in this novel, not further silencing them, but integrating their presence in a way that requires no battle. They are because they exist. Additionally, Walker addresses the foundation of this silence as outlined by hooks. In her essay "Homophobia in Black Communities," hooks posits that "clearly, religious beliefs and practices in many black communities promote and encourage homophobia. Many black folks (like other Christians in this society) are taught in churches that it is a sin to be gay, ironically sometimes by ministers who are themselves gay or bisexual" (122).[7] In revision, Walker creates an all-loving God, inserting female sexual desire into narratives of diaspora politic.

The position of religion and the role of God in their journey to self make Celie and Shug compelling versions of female sexuality. While Celie seems never to have psychologically complied with compulsory heterosexuality, Shug seems never to have been bridled by it, though she is fully heterosexually active. Mae Henderson explains this contrast in terms of Shug's being "a self-invented character whose sense of self is not male-inscribed" (16). This self-inscription or sexless inscription allows Shug to not only love men and women, but also to believe that lesbian love is cherished by God. She explains her awakened sense of herself as a "feeling of being part of everything not separate at all," and this feeling parallels sexual stimulation, which she indicates by rubbing Celie's thighs (178). When Celie winces at the connection, Shug explains that God understands her need for love and the satisfaction her relationship with Shug provides:

> God loves all them feelings. That's some of the best stuff God did. And when you know God loves 'em you enjoys 'em a lot more. You can just relax, go with everything that's going on, and praise God by liking what you like.
>
> God don't think it dirty? I ast.
>
> Naw, she say. God made it. Listen, God love everything you love—and a mess of stuff you don't. But more than anything else, God love admiration.
>
> You saying God vain? I ast.
>
> Naw, she say. Not vain, just wanting to share a good thing. I think it pisses God off if you walk by the color purple in a field somewhere and don't notice it. (178)

I quote this passage at length because it encapsulates the novel's representation of female homosexuality. First, the invocation of the novel's title informs us of the centrality of the lesbian relationship to an understanding of the narrative. As Hoogland indicates, "the colors violet and lavender have a history of association with lesbianism that goes as far back as 600 BC, to the poet Sappho and her female lovers who reputedly wore violet tiaras in their hair" (13). As well, purple is both a royal and holy color, a symbol of Christ's passion.[8] With this merging, Walker revises the royalty of the Holy Trinity, a trinity revised as Celie, Shug, and Albert, a continuous relationship, with no privileging of the male as God, the Father. Instead, we have a sexless God, who "don't look like nothing," for "It ain't something you can look at apart from anything else, including yourself . . . God is everything" (178). Given such a God, and within such a frame, Walker cannot insist on the subversive politics of Celie's lesbianism any more than she can posit Shug's bisexuality as oppressive, for the simultaneous existence of both these women's sexuality and the contact with each other *is* the subversive power of the narrative.

Whisper across the Void, or Let's Talk about Sex

Just as Walker revises notions of God, Cliff tells a new tale about female homosexuality while challenging the discourse that marks female homosexuality as perversely about a rejection of men.[9] Paul Gilroy tells us that the "telling and retelling" of the "narratives of loss, exile, journeying" serve to direct the attention of black peoples to some original mythic place in their social history (*Black Atlantic* 198). Even though Michelle Cliff claims that "Bertha Rochester is [Clare's] ancestor," connecting her to the histories recorded in the nineteenth-century novel *Jane Eyre* and marking her ancestry as in some ways profoundly English, she seems to be a photographic negative of Nella Larsen's Clare Kendry (Cliff, "Clare Savage" 265).[10] While Kendry passes for white, struggling to maintain ties to blackness, and has overtly erotic fantasies about her closest friend Irene Redfield, Clare Savage struggles to claim biological and sexual hybridity through her relationship with both Zoe and Harry/Harriet.[11] However, as Clare struggles to reconcile her mixed biology, she recognizes the value of her color, and as she turns tragedy into agency, she manipulates a sense of self-awareness.

In *Abeng,* Clare reads Charles Dickens's *Great Expectations,* and through this reading she discovers that not only is she racially divided, but also sexually divided. She tells us that while Dickens comes from "England" and "everyone there is white," nevertheless, England is Jamaica's mother country (36). Here, the relationship between white mother and dark-skinned child represents a clear inversion of the colonized explanation for the "mulatta" condition: the ravaging white father and victimized dark-skinned mother who births the light-skinned child. More important to this discussion, Clare highlights the ambiguity in terms of sexual definition as she identifies with Pip. Perhaps Clare's reading the story with herself as Pip could arguably be evidence that all women are taught to read as men, as Culler claims (43–64). However, Cliff complicates such a simple analysis later, when Clare is equally drawn to each of the suspected philanthropists, the unmarried white woman Miss Havisham and the darker convict Abel Magwitch, which directs our attention to her darker mother and her lighter father. Through this inversion, Clare's identification with a white woman and a dark man, Cliff highlights the newness of her narrative and the diaspora relationship that she wishes to engage, an inversion of certain sexual narratives. Most notably, she unwrites discourses that construct homosexuality as the result of *something,* for as Harry/Harriet says, rape "didn't make me who I am" (*No Telephone* 128).

Cliff assembles reflective images of racial and sexual duality in *Abeng* with Clare and Zoe's obviously homoerotic relationship, and with Clare's friendship with Harry/Harriet in *No Telephone to Heaven*. Like her namesake Clare Kendry, Clare Savage revels in the racial opposition that Zoe represents— though class difference is at work, as well, as I indicated in chapter 3. The narrator describes Zoe not only as Clare's "closest friend," but intimately so, in that "when the wispy hairs began to grow between Clare's legs and under her arms—slowly slowly—it was only Zoe she told, only Zoe she showed them to. And Zoe showed her own hairs" (*Abeng* 81). Furthermore, not only are they each other's mirrors of an awakening genderized/sexualized body, but their relationship is mostly cast in adolescent girl frolicking; it is within this frame that Cliff annotates a natural narrative of female homosexual development. After Clare and Zoe solve the dispute over the bathing suits, Clare places a "flame red hibiscus . . . behind Zoe's left ear," making Zoe the princess and she the prince (*Abeng* 101).

The sexual tensions of this moment are elucidated in concert with Celie's description of her vagina as a "wet rose." As well, as Celie claims maleness at the moment she feels her "nipples harden" and her "little button sort of perk up" at the sight of Shug (*Color Purple* 82), Clare is claiming a male model for herself. Refusing to be the passive princess waiting, she becomes the agential and active prince. This pattern of male identification is related to two familial realities. First, Kitty "handed her over to Boy" at birth, assuming the "light- skinned child [was] the child of the whitest parent" (*Abeng* 128–29). This absenting of herself from Clare's life parallels the physical death of Celie's mother and reinstitutes mother absence as a significant facet of these women's developing sexual lives. As well, Kitty positions herself as "quiet, in her marriage and motherhood" (129).

Lacking her mother, Clare has Zoe. Like Celie and Shug's secret intimacies, Zoe and Clare's secrecy includes menstruation and its connection to developed sexual bodies. Anxious and somewhat fearful, Clare ponders whether or not the absence of her menstrual cycle negatively marks her in some way. Her desire for her cycle is paralleled to her desire for Zoe. However, unlike Celie, physical sexual excitement is a secret that Clare keeps to herself: "Clare never asked Zoe whether she stroked herself in her pussy or across her chest or squeezed her own nipples. There were places in her parents' house Clare could do this secretly—but Zoe lived in one room with her mother and sister" (*Abeng* 107). Highlighting the boundary that class places on sexual exploration, her parents' wealth and stature afford her the space and place to come to these sexual awarenesses. Clare never reveals to Zoe the pleasure she experiences from these things and "the salty taste of her own moisture" (107). Clare's self-censorship signals that she is aware of the intense homophobia that surrounds her, so adolescent Clare defines herself within a paradigm set by Boy, indeed in terms of color and class, but also in terms of sex.

In order to justify her feelings to Zoe, she must thrive as Boy's child, socially male. This male identification explains the rage she feels when the boys, Joshua and Ben, exclude her from the game of their maleness. Clare recognizes this as a homosocial interaction and assigns the boys the power that such contracts warrant within kinship systems. However, the significance of her rage is intensified, for excluded by the homosociality of maleness, she recalls feeling "a distinct separation from women" (*Abeng* 61). Clare is dislocated from both men and women, a separation further highlighted when she and Zoe hunt the wild pig.[12] Zoe explains that Clare's obsession with the pig is, in fact, male, as what separates girls from boys is that the latter "[d]em like fe catch wild t'ings" (119). Clare concedes that she should abandon this boyish adventure, and she and Zoe "stripped off their clothes and splashed naked" in the river (119).

Naked reveling is also masculine behavior, for Clare had seen "Ben and Joshua do the same thing"; and because *boys* would swim naked in the river, Clare's grandmother forbade her to go there alone. Furthermore, Clare recalls that she has never seen another girl naked, "besides her little sister" and even in "her baths in this same place with Kitty each had been clothed" (*Abeng* 120). Gazing upon a female body satisfies her desire for maleness and her blossoming sexual desire for Zoe, similar to Celie's stirring when she first sees Shug Avery naked.

As Celie and Shug's body sharing leads them to intimacy, Zoe and Clare finish the swim by lying with "their bodies stretched against each other supported by grey and ancient rock," "closed their eyes," and "touched hands" (*Abeng* 120). The imagery of this scene foreshadows Clare's revelation that on the rock that day "she wanted to lean across Zoe's breast and kiss her . . . Just to say she was sorry" (124). The narrative representation of Clare's friendship with Zoe recalls that blurred line in adolescence between friend and lover— we learn how to be lovers in adulthood through our friendships in adolescence (Rich 24). Pointedly, this scene is immediately followed by Clare's recollection of her obligations under compulsory heterosexuality and the consequent homophobia that surrounds her.

Contemplating what losing Zoe's friendship would mean to her, Clare remembers her uncle Robert, whom the family ambivalently refers to as "funny," and his return from America in the company of a black American man he introduced as his "dearest friend" (*Abeng* 124). Robert rejects the friend's invitation to return to America so that the two "could make a home together," and Clare learns that "funny" means Robert is "a battyman—him want fe lay don wit only other men" (125). Outwardly, Clare developed a homophobic fear of Robert, refusing to talk with him. Then she remembers how he died. Robert, like Clinton, another villager accused of homosexuality and shunned because of it, swam out into the Kingston Harbor and drowned himself. He becomes a model for Clare when she realizes the depth of her feelings for Zoe, yet because they were girls, "funny," "off," and "queer" did not apply, for these referred to "batty*men*." Introspectively, however, Clare ponders whether hers and Zoe's was a relationship to be "guarded from the family" (127). Though their secrets are color-coded—loving someone darker—the secrecy is based on a fear that she will become a less viable subject for/to/within her family. Her relationship with Zoe is cast in homosexual contexts, and the "repellently homophobic" attitude of her relations clearly names homosexuality as "a malady [that] could ruin entire families" (Cliff, qtd. in Schwartz 599; *Abeng* 131).

The secrecy of their relationship is confirmed when Clare reports the accidental shooting of the bull, omitting Zoe's presence and negatively responding to her grandmother's charge that Clare's deviant behavior results from Zoe's encouraging her into it. The conversation with her grandmother highlights, as well, Clare's awareness of the inappropriateness of female homosocial contracts. Mattie further inscribes Clare's behavior as outside the realm of acceptable woman space, chastising her as "a girl who seemed to think she was a boy" (134). Clare inhabits a doubly gendered space. She is physically female, but her social and sexual positionality, coming from her father's influence, marks her as peculiarly male.

Clare realizes that like the battymen who, according to lore, are homosexual not because they hate their mothers, but because they are "spoiled men whose mothers had not weaned them soon enough," her love for Zoe "was something of a need for her mother" (131). Here, Cliff enacts an inversion of pyschoanalytic master narratives. Adrienne Rich questions why psychoanalysis posits that female children should transfer their libidinal desires from the original object mother to father. Clare also indicates that psychoanalysis depends upon *should,* or a compulsion, and does not elucidate a necessarily natural progression.

Clare owns female homosexual desire in this moment, capturing Butler's notion of the ambivalence of "being a man" and "being a woman" and highlighting the internal instability of each endeavor (*Bodies That Matter* 126). As well, Cliff refutes the notion of female (or male, for that matter) homosexuality as deviant behavior, or misandry. Clare's love for Zoe develops from the natural course of their closeness and the social intimacy that marks their friendship. This conscription frames Cliff's complicated representation of diaspora sexuality, specifically her challenge to the gendered divide.

Indeed, Boy's warning that Clare avoid boys, lest she become "ruined," ushers Clare not only into Zoe's confidence but also into the arms of Harry/Harriet, who, according to Cliff, is "the novel's lesbian . . . a man who wants to be a woman, and he loves women" (qtd. in Schwartz 605). Clare's adult relationship with Harry/Harriet is quite compelling, for it demonstrates an inversion of Walker's and Cliff's earlier representations of female heterosexuality. For Harry/Harriet, the issue is not a homosexual attraction, but some hybridization of the two: a biological male's heterosexual desire conflated with female gender identification. Harry/Harriet also reflects Cliff's interrogation of the relationship between sex and gender. Born a man, Harry/Harriet works as a medical officer but once served as a nurse, both gender-cast jobs. Described by an "old woman who penned Harriet's history" as "Mawu-Lisa, moon and sun, female-male deity," Harry/Harriet chooses to become Harriet, to ignore biology: "Harriet live and Harry be no more" (*No Telephone* 171, 168). Raped as a boy by a British officer, Harry/Harriet, like Shug to Celie, serves as a sexual identity gauge for Clare.

Harry/Harriet draws Clare back to Jamaica and back to the revolution that comprises most of *No Telephone to Heaven*'s narration. Mirroring Celie, the adult Clare returns to Jamaica with "a raging infection in her womb," which has made her sterile. Additionally, she is free of heterosexual ties, for her relationship with Bobby is over. He shared a secret that "he didn't need" to (*No Telephone* 128). While secrets cannot be shared within heterosexual contracts without severe consequences, homosocial contracts sustain and build on the divulging of secrets. In parallel to Shug and Celie's relationship, Clare discovers her attraction to Harry/Harriet when Harry reveals the secret of his rape, a secret kept to protect him from being "ruined" (129). "Feeling almost *womanly* in her sympathy," Clare confesses, "Harry, you make me want to love you" (130). This confession, couched in heterosexuality, shades that representation when Harry explains that by the rape, he "only suffered what [his] mother suffered," again marking Harry/Harriet as woman (129). Harry's marking himself as woman recalls Boy's choice of adjectives to describe a girl whose body has been exploited by men: ruined. These invocations revise *ruinate,* "a distinctive Jamaican term used to describe lands which were once cleared for agricultural purposes and have now lapsed back into . . . bush" (*No Telephone* 1). An adjective specifically defining land or a piece of territory becomes a referent to the gendered body, as well.

We are thus returned to the link between the body and territory, scripting diaspora women's bodies as fertile lands to be tilled by men, developed toward their nation-sustaining reproduction. However, Boy's message and Harry's rape intimate that only proper introduction into this particular market of purpose protects a body from ruination. Barren, Celie, Clare, and the divided Harry/Harriet must salvage their ruined bodies, for to engage in sex outside of heterosexual marriage, or, in fact, to be lesbian, is to become ruinate. Furthermore, the three must make a choice, "cast [their] lot," for as Harry/Harriet makes clear, one "cyann live split. Not in this world" (131). Choosing to live as woman resolves Harriet's dilemma, but as Clare is burned into the ground, we see the effects of the Jamaican whitewash. For the female homosexual, there is "no telephone to heaven."[13] The notion of woman's body as territory, though, recalls kinship narratives that emphasize reproduction as woman's revolutionary role. Walker creates a religious revolutionary who is able to embrace her sexuality.

However, Cliff's revolutionary dies without resolving the ambiguity of her sexual attraction. Ama Ata Aidoo, on the other hand, presents a nationalist activist whose experiences complicate Walker's resolution and explain Cliff's ambiguity. Just as Clare, seen reading a letter from Harry/Harriet informing her of how much "Jamaica needs her children," is told she looks "as if [she has] the weight of the world on her shoulders" (*No Telephone* 140), so does Sissie carry "Africa's problems on her shoulders" (*Killjoy* 118).

Sissie in Aidoo's *Our Sister Killjoy* takes a less directly developed course than her sisters. Yet she, like Celie and Clare, envisions herself male when confronted with her own passion for another woman. The prosetic novel details the experiences of Sissie, a Ghanaian woman traveling abroad in Europe. The text itself captures the hybridity of its subject—an educated African abroad—in its form, evoking the linearity of European narrative in its prose while maintaining the orality of African verse in the poetry. Like Clare's, Sissie's stay in London awakens her from the exile's dream: "to lose [themselves] in the [European world via] a naive faith that is a way to escape the feelings" of distinct senses of home and here (Dorsinville 63). Sissie rejects that London, or England, could ever be her colonial home. Her entire journey highlights the ways in which colonialism has cannibalized the history of her homeland, and Aidoo seizes "the initiative on Africa's behalf to make a timely intervention into the discourses that a European cultural apparatus writes over her homeland" (Korang 52). Though Sissie has no film to protest, she nonetheless works within the nationalist discourse of sexuality. As Wilentz notes, Sissie examines "the West's societal degeneration" as manifested in "the breakdown of the family" ("Politics of Exile" 83). However, as the family is related to bridled female sexuality, Sissie's experiences become especially significant.

Sissie's trip is occasioned by her unspecified role in her home government, an unusual role for a woman. Her journey also takes her to Frankfurt, where she meets "a young mother pushing her baby in a pram" through the park (*Killjoy* 19). She approaches Sissie and inquires of her race; this inquiry begins the relationship between Sissie and Marija Sommer, a housewife and mother to a son, Little Adolf. After a brief conversation about names, Marija bluntly announces, "I like to be your friend, yes?" and Sissie, intrigued by the young woman, answers affirmatively. Their friendship revolves around their mutual loneliness—Sissie for home and Marija for her tirelessly working husband, Big Adolf—and their recognition and belief in the importance of people, for "a long time ago people was all people had" (28). The friendship begins with Marija's desire to host Sissie's stay in Frankfurt. She promises to collect Sissie daily from the castle/youth hostel for tours of the city that end with dinner at her home. Each outing ends with Marija giving Sissie a ceremonial bag of plums.

Indeed, this section of the novel is entitled "The Plums," a European delicacy foreign in Ghana, forecasting the exotic attraction the two women share. Indicatively, the first gift of plums entrances Sissie, as she has never seen them before, and she is, indeed, "fascinated by the character of Marija's plums" and is equally pleased that Marija has selected the plums especially as a gift to her (40). Specifically, Sissie realizes that what makes the plums appealing is that they have certain "qualities that she herself possessed":

"Youthfulness / Peace of mind / Feeling free: / Knowing you are a rare article, / Being / Loved" (40). Sissie sat in Marija's company and ate the plums, "her tongue caressing the plump berries with skin colour almost like her own" (40). The erotic sensory images of this passage are constructed as a parallel to the city itself, and it serves to underscore Sissie's attraction to Marija. Through the gift of plums, Marija enacts a homosocial contract with Sissie and situates their relationship within a narrative of naturalness.

Revealing the connection between kinship and desire, at the hostel Sissie reflects on the romance-inspiring environment within which she finds herself:

An ancient ruined castle at the edge of a
Brooding pine forest, on the
Bank of a soft flowing river that
Sparkles silver
Under the late-night
Sun?

and the subsequent "hand-holding [and] wet-kissing" (41) this romantic setting always leads to. Her own time "under the late-night sun" always ends with her return to the hostel, alone, with plums in hand, a sign of Marija's presence. As well, the imagery conjures notions of the ruinate, symbolizing the geographic location of women's sexual desires, secreted within a forest of hairs. That Sissie savors the fruit in this space underscores that the plums are a signifier of homoerotic desire between her and Marija. They invoke, in flesh and texture, Walker's vision of a black woman's vagina as "the color of raspberries and blackberries—or scuppernongs and muscadines" (*In Search* 374).

Just as Sissie is fascinated by the exotic plums, she herself is an exotic fixture, "a crowd getter," for in Lower Bavaria "the mere presence of an African girl is phenomenal" (43). Moreover, Sissie adds to her intrigue by always being seen in the company of Marija, "a little housewife married to a factory hand" (43). As is true for Clare and Zoe, class and color separate Sissie and Marija, as well. A flurry of gossip begins among the "thinned-out end of the old aristocracy and those traditional lickers of aristocratic arse" over how it was that "it was not them or their wives escorting the African Miss" (44). Indeed, they reason that something is afoul. Their color difference, a silence between them in the same way that both of these issues are between Clare and Zoe, is spoken by an older German couple they encounter on one of their daily walks. The man points to his and Sissie's arms, commenting furiously in German. Neither's comments are translated, but the encounter kills Sissie's excitement over Marija's promise of a plum cake. However, Sissie makes a clear sexual connection with Marija, and like Celie and Clare, she thinks herself male, for this is the only way for her to love another woman:

> Once or so, at the beginning of their relationship, Sissie had thought . . . what a delicious love affair she and Marija would have if only one of them had been a man. Especially if she, Sissie had been a man. (61)

But she also realizes, as Clare learns about the hunt, that her flirtations were "[a] game in which one day, she became absorbed, she forgot who she was, and the fact that she was a woman" (61).

Furthermore, Sissie, like Clare and Celie (who, through Shug, attaches to her mother), recalls the images of hand-holding and wet-kissing, and foreshadows such an exchange between Marija and herself: "Sissie thought of home. To the time when she was a child in the village. . . . Oo, to be wrapped up in a mother's cloth while it rained. Every time it rained" (64). Sissie is reminded that she is a woman, and for this reminder she does not give Marija a ceremonial hibiscus, or comb her hair out, but she announces that she must leave; however, first she has to say good-bye to the child.

This linking between motherhood and homosocial contracts indicates the continuum on which female homosexuality resides. As Sissie makes her way to the boy's room, the stairs become an escalator "down into some primeval cave" (*Our Sister Killjoy* 64), the pit where blackwomen's homosexual desires have fallen (E. White 45).[14] Paralleling Celie and Shug, in the middle of Marija's "nuptial chamber," the two women kiss. While Clare can only imagine connecting with Zoe across the lines of color and class, Sissie and Marija bridge that impasse, briefly: "Sissie felt Marija's cold fingers on her breast. The fingers of Marija's hand touched the skin of Sissie's breasts while her other hand groped round and round Sissie's midriff for something to hold on to" (64). Sissie is shaken by this exchange, the encounter with the old couple, her memory of a desire to be male, and other events that question the legitimacy of their relationship. That is, Sissie reflects on the nationalistic detriment that such a relationship can foster. Sissie is transplanted to a killjoy memory that, like Clare's recollection of her cousin Robert's experience, refocuses her relationship with Marija. Sissie sees her desires as not only a potential source of shame for herself and her family, but also as further evidence of Europeans' negative influences on the African psyche.

Walker notes that "there have been people on earth who didn't think about sex the way white Western" people did (qtd. in E. White 45). Similarly, Sissie recalls an incident at her boarding school that made expressly clear that if she were one of these people, such ideas about sex were not allowed. Sissie's head-mistress's spirit was broken when "one night, on one of her regular nocturnal inspections, she found two girls in bed together" (66). Just as Clare parallels herself with the ruinate, facing the possibility that her body will return to bush, Sissie is asked, as a child, if she is bush. Furthermore, "from knowledge gained since," Sissie understands that two women in bed together, an inevitable result of their loving, was "not just b-u-s-h / But a C-r-i-m-e / A Sin / S-o-d-o-m-y" (67). As such, I take issue with Wilentz's reading that Sissie rejects Marija in favor of heterosexuality ("Politics of Exile" 84). Instead, I see Sissie's anguish as related to notions of race and family, and I read her response as an attempt to reconcile the role of nationalist women with their identities as female homosexuals.[15] Faced with this context, Sissie, like her narrative sisters, is forced to wish "she was a boy. A man" and to mourn the loss of potential lovers (67).

To further avert her feelings, Sissie insults Marija by first canceling a date with her to have dinner with her family—Big Adolf included—and then by informing Marija that she has a boyfriend. Marija's perceived jealousy is met by Sissie's pleasure in obviously hurting her. Her imagined maleness returns and "hit her like a stone," that "masculine delight that is exhilarating beyond all measure" (76).

Though the narrator gives us Sissie's pleasure at Marija's pain, it is equally valid that these tears Marija sheds allow Sissie to once again have intimacy with Marija. These tears recreate the moment of the impassioned embrace when Marija's tears landed warmly on Sissie's neck. Just as she at that moment had settled into her prescribed female self, Sissie does so here, as well, reminding Marija that "it is not sound for a woman to enjoy cooking for another woman. Not under any circumstances. . . . Special meals are for men. They are the only sex to whom the Maker gave a mouth with which to enjoy eating" (77). Marija sadly concedes, but she makes a final gesture when she rush-es to meet Sissie's early morning train to say goodbye. With "one suspicious tear already glistening the lashes of the left eye," Marija gives Sissie a brown bag complete with various food items and a final gift of plums, a sign of their homosocial contract (78, 82). This final gift (re)inscribes the erotic/exotic desire that defined their relationship and indicates that women can enjoy the delectable fruits of other women's labor. This pleasure is not the exclusive province of heterosexual (or even heterosocial) contracts.

Celie, Clare, and Sissie evince the struggle to create a space within which female homosexual desire can be articulated. Their desire for maleness captures this struggle and their recognition of their own conscription, for as Jane Flax posits,"[a]ll speaking beings 'inscribe themselves' on the masculine side, no matter what their physical attributes may be. To speak, one must enter into and be constituted by the realm of the symbolic—the play of signifiers and the signified and 'the universal signifier' (the phallus). Those who would lack access to the phallus and hence to the world . . . are called 'woman'" (111). Such character casting demonstrates the interstices between sexuality, gender, race, and class, for in black nationalist discourse, the silencing of women, and the privileging of the phallus, becomes more insidious as it is related to the very struggle of black men and women to save their own lives. The desire to be male highlights and inverts this dictum, for these women who would be men maintain their roles as warriors, Clare in the resistance and Sissie when she returns to Ghana intent on using what she has learned to further their national growth. As well, Celie is a warrior exerting economic power and rewriting Monique Wittig's claim that "lesbians are not women," given that "'woman' has meaning only in heterosexual systems of thought and heterosexual economic systems" (110).

Narrating Women's Sexuality: A Family Affair

Walker's *By the Light of My Father's Smile* bridges the gap between Cliff's Clare and Aidoo's Sissie, and represents Walker's cautious listening to the voices of her diaspora sisters. Caught at the confluence of two worldviews, Magdalena is neither a revolutionary nor a daughter taken in by her father's dogma on female behavior. Like Celie, Magdalena first engages in heterosexual sex before realizing her lesbian desires. In stark contrast, however, each of the characters discussed so far reveals a certain mother lack that stands as the basis for their sexual desires: "The saddest part is always when the mother dies, which she tends to do early in the story. We are always grateful that she goes early, because it is so hard to lose her; it is far better to have her death behind us rather than in front of us, as we trudge off to meet our destiny" (*By the Light* 128). In Magdalena's case, as in Tashi's, the absence of mother(s) precludes her discovery of women's inability to protect their daughters from the power of men. Nonetheless, the axis for Magdalena's sexual narrative is her father. The novel opens with her involved in a full-blown lesbian affair. However, we learn that she comes to love women only after being severely punished by her father for making love with a Mundo boy. Like Boy Savage's policing of Clare through warning against being ruined, Magdalena's father beats her barbarically for engaging in a noncontractual sexual exchange.

Highlighting the intersection between kinship models and excising critical inquiry into blackwomen's sexuality, *By the Light* explores how nationalist attitudes toward female sexuality damage men, women, and even nation. The novel focuses on the lives of two sisters, Susannah and Magdalena, but Magdalena, Mad Dog, later June, is the primary protagonist. The novel takes the multiple narrative form of *Possessing*, but more complicatedly so. The narration is at times in the first person—Susannah or Magdalena, or their dead father, who, in the tradition of the Mundo, returns to "guide back to the path (of death) someone [he] has left behind who is lost, because of [his] folly" and "to host a ceremony so that [he] and others [he] has hurt may face eternity reconciled and complete" (*By the Light* 148). Just as Cliff provides the Savage genealogy in *Abeng*, over the course of *By the Light* we learn the Robinson family's history alongside the history of the Walker-created Mundo, "a band of people who are neither African nor Indian, but a blend" (E. White 46). Furthering the writer-as-anthropologist mode so clearly evidenced in *Possessing*, we have the Robinsons, whose patriarch, a pastor, has taken the family to "splendid isolation in Sierra Madre," because the father's church "sent [him] as spiritual advisor to Mexico to work among the Mundo" (*By the Light* 15, 14). Passing himself off as an anthropologist and fraudulently acquiring grant monies to support himself and his family, he and the family settle into the tribe. But, breaking the anthropological tradition of participant-observer, the father forbids his family certain kinds of contact with the Mundo. While Susannah and Langley—"enthralled by the [Mundo] women's serene mastery of their craft"—"studied pottery with the women," Magdalena busied herself with "the wild Indian boys," learning "how to run, as they did, like the wind" (18). Like Clare and Celie, Magdalena wishes to fashion herself male.

Magdalena's fashioning is problematized by not only the patriarchal and nationalist values the father represents but also by his Christianity. Similar to Boy Savage's warning to Clare against ruination and Sissie's invocation of the responsibility of African women to their nation, Mr. Robinson pleads with his wife to explain to Maggie why she can no longer run like the wind in the company of the boys. Mr. Robinson fears that his daughter will engage in heterosexual contracts not sanctioned by himself and not furthering the outlined goals of nationalist sexuality. However, signaling the validity of homosocial contracts and deriding the inherently male and heterosexual privileging that her husband implies, Langley explains, "it does not seem to me that Mad Dog wishes to sleep with anyone, other than with her sister" (19).

However, Magdalena does engage in sex with Manuelito, and she incurs a severe beating. The beating marks her as ruinate territory, a whore whose father is no longer able to indulge her anything. Undermining the sanctity with which fathers grant such indulgence, Walker demonstrates how the tenets of compulsory heterosexuality violate men's and women's freedoms and as such have the potential to destroy, not build strong, healthy nations.

The patience and caring of Manuelito's lovemaking contrasts with Mr. Robinson's response. To forbid Manuelito to see his daughter is not enough; he has to tarnish both the memory of her lovemaking and the spirit of her partner. Walker makes clear that Manuelito violates the rules of economy when he does not ask Mr. Robinson's permission. The viability of any kinship system requires that men recognize each other's powers and the boundaries of their territories. But what the father learns in death is that he traversed an even more sacred boundary and turned to ruin even more precious territory. Not only did the beating scar Magdalena and prevent her from loving her father, but "he [was] never again permitted to really know or enjoy his favorite little tree," his other daughter Susannah, who peeps through the key-hole and witnesses the beating. In a show of true sistered kinship, Susannah allies herself with Magdalena, sharing her sister's pain. Mr. Robinson learns, then, that any productive kinship must allow a space for women to express their sexual identity, for the consequences to family, the central focus of nationalist sexual politics, are dire.

With the adult Magdalena, and through the course of her relationship with Pauline, the father and daughter learn that "bad women aren't the only women" who have and enjoy sex (126). Though the novel's sexual narrative is complicated by the blending of excessive themes and motifs (e.g., cultural exploitation, the Vietnam War), Walker furthers the representation of lesbian love that she began in *The Color Purple*. Led on his post-life journey by Manuelito, the father witnesses the frailty of his daughters, their insecurity in love, and the destiny he fashioned for them. He is most taken with Magdalena, for while she possesses the strongest presence as a child, she is also the most frail, and "her obesity is designed to hide this" (150). The father witnesses his daughter's sexual becoming. Overcoming his shock at her les-bianism allows Mr. Robinson to embrace his daughters' sexuality as necessary.

While Cliff, Aidoo, and Walker herself, in *The Color Purple*, use women protagonists to usher in a new version of black women's sexuality, here Walker shifts the focus to men. Her move is not to suggest that fathers are the point of departure for their daughters' sexual definition. Instead, Walker suggests that revising the compulsory heterosexuality that underwrites kinship systems is men's business, as well. Creating a space for female homosociality, sexual or not, does not undermine families but rather strengthens them.

In a textual moment that aptly captures my characterization, Susannah is writing a novel after a brief postmarital affair. The father notices that she is having difficulty writing in sex, so he intercedes with encouragement:

> Write it in, I screech from the celestial sidelines. Put the sex right up on in there! Even if it's nothing but the copulating dogs you saw from your window as a five-year-old when we lived in Mexico. . . . It's not so big a deal! I want her to know. As I see her, crippled in a place that should be free, and still after all these years, perplexed by the memory of her sister's stubborn face and the sound of the whistling silver belt. And my own face, what did she read there, what message about the consequences of a searing passion, ecstatic sex? (28)

That he associates Susannah's reluctance to embrace her sexuality with Magdalena's punishment for sexual revelry illustrates both processes by which women are sexually imprinted by societal messages.

Susannah learns from his response to her sister what is appropriate behavior, and she becomes a sexually silenced woman. As well, the mention of the dogs in Mexico recalls Magdalena's desire to be called "Mad Dog," after the wise species the Mundo appreciate who "lose their minds," as a symbol of how important it is to "not live too much in your head. It is a way of reminding you to stay with your emotions . . . a way of saying, also, that craziness has value" (93).

Realizing that he has lived too much in his head, depended too much on a notion of kinship that excises women's sexual beings, the father comes to see himself as a necessary presence in his daughters' sexual lives. He comes to "know how deeply [his] daughters are wounded by [his] apparent incomprehension (in life) that [his] daughters [had] sexual feelings" (E. White 47). The father realizes that Magdalena's mad behavior, her running with the wind, her physical desire for and emotional commitment to Manuelito, all made her his daughter. He is finally able to embrace Magdalena as both "mad dog and his sane daughter" (*By the Light* 19).

In this scene, Walker parallels the power men receive in a system that makes women social property with the elation that Mr. Robinson exhibits as he encourages Susannah to not only acknowledge her sexual desires but also to give them a clear place in her story. She asks her readers to imagine, as she does, a people who accept the sexual behaviors of their daughters as natural and self-directed. Recognizing the difficulty of unlearning compulsory heterosexuality, Walker's Mr. Robinson witnesses both of his daughters coming to sexual life, but his faith in the sanctity of heterosexual contracts still haunts him. Hesitant to participate in their sexual lives, he questions the legitimacy of his "[t]rying to have a place in an area I had nearly destroyed. " Manuelito informs him that it is not only natural but also necessary, for the dead "return to spy on the confusion" of the living, "to weave [a] story" that gives that confusion logic (149, 150). The story that Mr. Robinson weaves is one that erases the confusion created by the strident homophobia that Clare's family projects, manifested in Sissie's willingness to ignore her sexual passions in fulfillment of her nationalist obligations.

The trajectory from Walker's Mr. Robinson to Cliff's Harry/Harriet manifests an excavation of sexuality that leads them both to a new understanding, the father of his daughters and Harry/Harriet of his destiny as a lesbian lover of women. Celie, Shug, and Sissie manifest the depths of diaspora women's bonding, demonstrating the links between their kinship and their sexuality. Though *By the Light of My Father's Smile* concludes with a reconciled father, its message is clear that the reconciliation prefaces any sustainable kinship system. Aidoo, Cliff, and Walker construct a nationalist, diaspora, or kinship politic that acknowledges the diversities of histories and experiences that link the members of the system.

The male intellectual emphasis on the race-as-family model has left women particularly silent. Male-centered diaspora narratives have underwritten the role of women as well as the effect of homosocial contracts between men. The revolutionary women presented in this chapter demonstrate an inversion of nationalist power. They propose a kinship system that recognizes the intellectual, social, and (re)productive values of all its members. In this, Walker, Cliff, and Aidoo usher in a new diaspora politic and consciousness of kinship; they have unpacked theory to create a pragmatic foundation for a nationalist conversation with their brothers and sisters about the power of their sisterhood. That all three writers have their women envision themselves as men reflects how they invert the homosocial order that privileges male social, intellectual, political, and fictional contracts.

Afterword:
Bridging the Middle Passage

bridge: structure carrying a pathway or roadway over a depression or obstacle; a time, place, or means of connection or transition; a musical passage linking two sections of a song.

Understanding the "difference place makes" made a *bridge* the only logical chronotope for the analyses I undertake in this book. In form, Michelle Cliff's writing bridges the distance between Alice Walker's work and Ama Ata Aidoo's literature. African Americans have dominated diaspora inquiry, and Alice Walker's journey reveals the "complicated politic" of engineering diaspora identity (Olaniyan 536). She grounds her politic in a conversation between black peoples, specifically Africans and African Americans. Walker's fiction acknowledges that these conversations sometimes articulate "mutually contradictory and often antagonistic elements" (Olaniyan 536). Introducing Cliff's narratives exposes the antagonistic elements in previous notions of the diaspora and the race family. Cliff highlights that a diaspora studies that confines itself to analyzing the lives and experiences of *black* people is limited and contradictory. Black Africans and African Americans must acknowledge and address their Creole cousins, if the fiction of the diaspora is to reflect its geographic reality. In turn, Aidoo makes it difficult to talk about *the* African woman; she refuses to allow any deification of African women as either ur-mother or ur-sister.

These women's writings become a metaphor for their geographic locations, and their locations in the books recall the places of their homelands along the journey that created the diaspora (the transatlantic slave route or the Middle Passage). However, this book reverses the historical passage, manifesting the directional route of diaspora inquiry as it moves back toward the source. Walker's United States is my contemporary homeland and my intellectual point of departure. Cliff's Jamaica serves as a port of call, a transitional stop en route to our destination, Aidoo's Ghana—the symbolic home and the historical motherland. The bridge metaphor extends beyond the book's form, however. Functionally, the writers and their writing bridge the Middle Passage. Their invocations of a sunken history, and their dialogue across and through the gaps and tensions that absence creates, yield an alternative framework for diaspora inquiry. The conversation between these women redesigns the diaspora, and the bridge underscores that for each diaspora child, there are at least two cultural sensibilities. These three women make critical space for and give narrative voice to a once muted kinship song.

Though Walker, Cliff, and Aidoo have been heralded for their women-directed narratives, I relocate their fiction, providing another context within which to read and evaluate their writing and gendered politic. I refocus analyses of each woman's work to how each writes female agency and subjectivity into the diaspora narrative. My readings of Walker, Cliff, and Aidoo open up their particular texts while demonstrating that diaspora studies must expand. Once driven by an intellectual tendency toward origin mapping, diaspora inquiry must attend equally to the pragmatic realities of location, color and class, gender and sexuality. Walker, Aidoo, and Cliff take the existence of the diaspora—as an intellectual and sociocultural space—for granted. Their goal is not to argue its boundaries. Instead, each examines the consequences of diasporization, emphasizing that the syncretism that frames any notion of the diaspora manifests itself in a slight elision of the boundary between fiction and reality. These writers engage the fiction of the race family, born in the early days of Pan Africanism. Attentive to the material and lived realities of women and men, Walker's, Cliff's, and Aidoo's writings reveal the varied experiences of dispersed people who have made a life from the cultural, social, political, and geographic raw materials of the spaces they inhabit.

Using their fiction, I have crafted a genealogy that reveals how orphanage is a metaphor for diaspora relations, equally as powerful as—if not more so than—family. An alternative kinship system that embraces displacement and relocation, orphanage challenges the discourses of identity and truth. Each writer's literary work embraces the significance of difference in reifying the diaspora as a space that is evolving rather than static and fixed. We—the writers and I—offer diaspora consciousness, a critical lens that requires us to acknowledge that individual diaspora spaces have distinct historical narratives. Nonetheless, Walker, Cliff, and Aidoo negotiate across their differences, defy attempts to monolithicize, and exemplify an artistic, intellectual, and pragmatic posture informed by both affinity and dissonance.

As mi people dem say:
"Fa heal de tree, ya mus' take cyear a de root"

Diaspora inquiry has at its core the mending of a broken historical narrative, and its focus has been reconnecting the dispersed people to their roots. Diaspora consciousness does more than reaffirm Africa as an originating point, however. The continent becomes a site of inquiry within the larger diaspora landscape. Redefining the diaspora in this way replaces the objective of demonstrating where and how the African self latently resides within the relocated body. Diaspora consciousness foregrounds the negotiation of the cultural and material realities of life on the continents of Africa and North America and in the islands of the Caribbean for people of African descent. Most significantly, Walker and Cliff are unencumbered by the historical silences that Aidoo writes against. Walker writes Tashi, licensed by the voices of her ancestral muses. Cliff's Clare fights to the death to secure the legacy of her ancestral mother and the maroonage scripted by her narrative. But Aidoo struggles against a muted narrative, and her Anowa gives voice to the reality of the continent's silent diaspora history.

Both this book and the writers it examines represent a transition in diaspora studies, a move away from the theory of syncretism to the social, political, cultural, and artistic manifestations of diasporization. Each writer's work acquaints us with characters who struggle to know themselves, to be confirmed in their sense of themselves. These textual women represent the struggle of living women, who negotiate their limited agency within the "race family," and who write themselves out of separation anxiety and into a kinship system characterized as much by divergent ideological postures as by converging cultural practices.

My analysis begins a critical dialogue that must continue. Highlighting the importance of place, I instigate a significant paradigm shift in black diaspora cultural and literary studies. For example, writers like Beryl Gilroy, whose writing mediates the spaces of Britain and Guyana, would add another level of complexity to the notion of diaspora, given that the United States has no central place in her work. Diaspora consciousness widens the field of inquiry in terms of language, as well. An integration of literature from the French-speaking Caribbean and Africa into diaspora conversations is wanting. Reading Maryse Condé's narratives through the lens of diaspora consciousness could further redefine diaspora projects. Including French-speaking places and French textual spaces would provoke an examination of the relationship between diaspora consciousness and postcoloniality.

The Difference Place Makes was designed to explore three women's writers' voices and offer them as examples of a revision of a diaspora politic. As the study of African diaspora literature—falling under the rubric of various interdisciplinary projects such as black studies, diaspora studies, black Atlantic studies, diaspora cultural studies, and other variations of the theme—broadens, the fictive worlds of women writers hold much upon which to build a theory of black narrative. In this way, I offer this book and its critical study as a bridge into a new paradigm for diaspora studies. Moving away from past versions of Pan African sensibilities toward diaspora consciousness, *The Difference Place Makes* directs its readers to new structures, voices, spaces, and places in a broadened diaspora studies.

notes

Notes to Preface

1. For detailed discussion of the Gullah's preserved vestiges of African culture, see John Henrik Clarke, foreword to *Sea Island Roots,* Mary A. Twining and Keith A. Baird, eds. (Trenton, N.J.: African World Press, 1991), v–vi; and Lorenzo Dow Turner's seminal study, originally published in 1949, *Africanisms in the Gullah Dialect* (Ann Arbor: University of Michigan Press, 1974). Also see Patricia Jones Jackson's *When Roots Die: Endangered Traditions in the Sea Islands* (Athens: University of Georgia Press, 1987), where my great-grandfather, Richard Linen [*sic*], appears on the cover.

Notes to Chapter 1

1. This title is a play on the Zora Neale Hurston essay "How It Feels to Be Colored Me," in *I Love Myself When I Am Laughing and Then Again When I'm Looking Mean and Impressive,* ed. Alice Walker (Old Westbury, N.Y.: Feminist Press, 1979), 152–55.

2. The distinction that I am making between the references "black women" and "blackwomen" is one of representation. "Black women" refers to women of African descent in the United States, while "blackwomen" refers to women of African descent throughout the world, including but not limited to the United States.

3. Here I am distinguishing between Afrocentric scholars who focus almost exclusively on (re)situating Africa as a central point in our histories and scholars who study the history of black people generally.

4. There were also numerous articles printed that discussed the merits of Afrocentric projects like those undertaken by Molefi Asante, and in one *Newsweek* article, Henry Louis Gates and Asante literally squared off on the same page (23 September 1991, 46–47). Gates's prominence provided fodder for seasoned discussion outside of mainstream literary circles, as well. Publications attempted to discredit his approach to black studies, favoring the approach termed Afrocentrist. Because these are all well beyond the scope of this particular project, I will not go into specific details.

5. For an in-depth analysis of the conflict(s) between black female and male theorists, see Adell's discussion in chapter 4 of her *Double Consciousness/Double Bind.* There Adell

analyzes feminist/womanist critiques of black male scholars as well as examines the critical consequences of such debate (90–117).

6. Here I want to note my varying capitalizations of the word "blackness." As rules for standard English usage tell us, capitalization indicates a certain way we should read and understand written language. Hence Blackness indicates a reference to, or discussion of, raced ideas while blackness refers to culture.

7. Note that contemporaneously with Frederick Douglass, Martin R. Delany was also writing and speaking on similar issues. However, Delany's objectives were quite different. Interestingly enough, the differences between Delany and Douglass resurfaced in the 1960s in the split between Martin Luther King, Jr.'s Southern Christian Leadership Conference (SCLC) and the more revolutionary organizations like the Student Nonviolent Coordinating Committee (SNCC) and the Black Panthers. For more on Delany, see Victor Ullman's *Martin R. Delany: The Beginnings of Black Nationalism* (Boston: Beacon Press, 1971); and Nell Painter's "Martin R. Delany: Elitism and Black Nationalism," in *Black Leaders in the Nineteenth Century,* eds. Leon Litwack and August Meier (Chicago: University of Illinois Press, 1987), 149–72.

8. See Mullin's *Africa in America,* 268–75.

9. Almost thirty years later, we get a travel novel that revisits Aidoo's thesis and reflects Echewa's, Williams's, and Killens's concerns. Eddy Harris, in his 1992 work *Native Stranger,* not only documents his journey to and from Africa, he also narrates a connection with his past. He concludes that he is "a product of a new culture and defined by it. And [he] sees the world through American eyes" (29). The routes of displacement have demanded a replanting of roots, and this (re)rooting cannot be eschewed.

10. I am speaking especially to Kwame Anthony Appiah's critique of Du Bois's ideas on race. Appiah argues that Du Bois's preoccupations with the concept of race reinforce biological notions of race, all while Du Bois claims to be actively struggling to only name African American identity. Appiah goes on to explain the connection between Du Bois's ideas on race and their intrinsic connection to ideas of nationalities, making nation "more and more [closely] identified as a biological unit, defined by a shared essence that flows from common descent" (51). While I agree that Du Bois ushers in the idea of race-as-nation, I disagree that this conflation is necessarily and/or solely biological. See Appiah's chapter on Du Bois, "The Illusion of Race," 28–46.

11. Of course, I discuss this in more detail in chapter 3; see Cliff's "Clare Savage as a Crossroads Character."

12. This reference to Dilthey as first defining or "naming" the hermeneutic circle is taken from my reading of Gadamer's *Truth and Method* (265).

13. What Esonwanne is suggesting is that there exists, or can exist, an interpretive community defined by and constructed by "race." But he is skeptical of readings that emerge from such an interpretive community because of their mythic center: "race."

14. Having defeated the Ashanti, the British annexed their lands in 1901. Present-day Ghana was the center of the Ashanti Empire, which had grown in both wealth and power between the thirteenth and nineteenth centuries. Formerly the British Gold Coast, after Nkrumah led it to independence, Ghana served as a model to other colonial nations. However, Nkrumah's reign became authoritarian, and poverty and corruption spread through the newly liberated nation. Nkrumah was deposed by military coup and exiled. He left what had been a wealthy country, in social discontent and in rapid economic

decline. For detailed discussions of the progress and retardation of Nkrumah's rule, see Henry Bretton's *The Rise and Fall of Kwame Nkrumah* (New York: Praeger, 1967); for the history of Ghana's colonization, see Robert Edgerton's *The Fall of the Ashanti Empire: The Hundred-Year War for Africa's Gold Coast* (New York: The Free Press, 1995).

15. Note Ranu Samantrai's "Caught at the Confluence of History: Ama Ata Aidoo's Necessary Nationalism," wherein Aidoo's *Our Sister Killjoy* is read as an unabashed appeal to "Africans' sense of loyalty and obligation to Africa," *Research in African Literatures* 26, no. 2 (1995): 140–57, quote on p. 142. This reading corresponds with my suggestion here that Aidoo is influenced by Nkrumah's political legacy. However, Samantrai—like Odamtten in his readings of Aidoo's work—relegates Aidoo's politics to her native Ghana, while I infer more far-reaching implications.

16. Raiskin aptly claims that this linguistic genealogy "casts the surrounding colonial vocabulary of nationality and racial identity into confusion" (3).

17. Using a "bridge" to frame and comment upon this project is much like Paul Gilroy's use of "ships" in his work *The Black Atlantic.*

18. See my "Slavery in the Diaspora Consciousness: Ama Ata Aidoo's Conversations," wherein I discuss the relationship between W. E. B. Du Bois's and Kwame Nkrumah's Pan Africanism, and I examine the manifestations of this politic in Aidoo's writings. *Emerging Perspectives on Ama Ata Aidoo,* eds. Ada Uzoamaka and Gay Wilentz (Terenton, N.J.: Africa New World, 1999), 27–44.

19. Though some male writers have addressed the dispersal of Africans during the slave trade, their response has not been as focal as Aidoo's. Wole Soyinka, for example, has an African American school artist, Joe Golder, in his *Interpreters,* and mentions Africans selling Africans during the slave trade in *A Dance of the Forests.* There is a mention of black Americans in Ngugi wa Thiong'o's *Devil on the Cross,* and Ayi Kwei Armah explores the experiences of black Americans traveling to Africa in his *Fragments* and *Two Thousand Seasons.* Syl Cheney Coker's *The Last Harmattan of Alusine Dunbar* centers around African Americans who have emigrated to Liberia. In film, Sembène Ousmane's *Ceddo* (1976) discusses the slave trade, and his *Camp de Thiaroye* (1987) brings an African and an African American face to face. Most recently, Armah investigates the relationship between Ghanaians and United States blacks in his *Osiris* (1994). Nonetheless, compared to African American writings on the historical connections between these two peoples, African discussion has been limited. See Berth Lindfors, "The Image of the Afro-American in African Literature," and Jacob Drachler's edited collection *Black Homeland/Black Diaspora* for further details.

20. With respect to African American women writers' constructs of African women, see also Maya Angelou's *All God's Children Need Travelling Shoes.* It is not my goal to argue that Walker is the only African American woman to "write" an African; Angelou offers another such writing. However, I have selected to focus on Walker specifically because of the didactic and polemical nature of her construction and the representational problems that her/story engenders.

21. It could very convincingly be argued that Aidoo and Emecheta's argument that African societies were not patriarchal is indicative of their own ideological approaches to reading gender in Africa. That is to say, I am in no way suggesting that their positions are reflective of all African women writers. Mariama Bâ and Ellen Kuzwayo create literature that reflects an alternate analysis of gender and colonialism, for example.

22. This notion of the exchange of women as a social contract between men is best exemplified in Walker's *The Color Purple* and in much of African women's fiction, particularly Buchi Emecheta's work. As well, Linda Abbandonato discusses Walker's engagement of this concept in her article "A View from 'Elsewhere'" (especially see pp. 1109–10).

23. There are several issues at play here. I want to emphasize that in traditional polygamous relationships this notion of male economy is interrupted by the participation of women in the selection of co-wives. As well, the co-wives then form a collective within both the public and private spheres that is exclusive of men. This female-centered homosociality may perhaps explain why Western ideologies, even feminist ones, are so strictly opposed to polygamy. See my critique of Esi in chapter 4 below; additionally, in chapter 5, I explore the quasi-polygamous relationship presented in *The Color Purple*.

24. Patricia Hill Collins in *Fighting Words* offers a very cogent and detailed analysis of these ideas of woman as mother and woman as nation, within the context of Afrocentric discourse. Her analysis intersects with mine here insofar as Afrocentrism is the child of Pan Africanism and a sibling to diaspora consciousness. See chapter 5, "When Fighting Words are Not Enough: The Gendered Content of Afrocentricism," 155–83.

25. I agree with Butler's observation that such an equation is reductive and "misses the specific histories of their construction and elaboration, but also delays the important work of thinking through the ways in which these vectors of power require each other for the purpose of their own articulation" (*Bodies That Matter* 18). See also bell hooks's "Homophobia in Black Communities," wherein she explains the ways in which black people read such conflations as "minimizing or diminishing the particular problems people of color face in a white-supremacist society, especially the problems encountered because one does not have white skin" (125). She concurs with Butler that we need analyses of the ways in which both of these liberation struggles inform each other.

Notes to Chapter 2

1. The film begins with a voice-over of this poem. It serves, as Sandra Grayson argues, to foreshadow Mona's transformational journey as a means through which "the spirits of the dead will tell their story" (214). Additionally, Walker says of her crafting *Possessing*, she felt she was speaking for her ancestors, indeed, hearing their voices. See "Alice Walker's Appeal."

2. It is worth noting here, however, that Walker's construction of one ancestor, M'Lissa, challenges the common notion of the ancestor as a consistently positive force (e.g., in Toni Morrison's "Rootedness"). While one should—must—look to the ancestor for guidance, the ancestor can direct one *against* certain behaviors. That is, the ancestor can be an example of a path one should not take.

3. I struggle with the language of naming and representations given in the names we choose. In keeping with the Gullah proverb that heads this chapter, I turn to the language provided by those whose lives are shaped by this ritual. I am fully aware, however, that to many readers "ritual female circumcision" will appear euphemistic; yet I have elected to use it in my discussion of the practice. Though Walker and many Western (and non-Western) critics use the more graphic "female genital mutilation," it is not my position to argue whether the operation is or is not mutilative. My choice of phrase represents an acknowledgment of its validity for those who adhere to it and struggle to defend and maintain the practice, a faction, in many ways, represented by the character Tashi herself.

4. The title of Walker's novel is taken from *African Saga,* the memoir of an Italian woman raised in Kenya: "I had always got on well with the Africans and enjoyed their company, but commanding the people on the farm, many of whom had watched [me] grow up. With the added experience of my safaris behind me, I had begun to understand the code of 'birth, copulation and death' by which they lived. Black people are natural, they *possess the secret of joy,* which is why they can survive the suffering and humiliation inflicted upon them. They are alive physically and emotionally, which makes them easy to live with. What I had not yet learned to deal with was their cunning and their natural instinct for self-preservation." Quoted in Alice Walker, *Possessing the Secret of Joy* (New York: Harcourt Brace, 1992). Interestingly, Walker paraphrases this excerpt for the paperback edition of *Possessing.* That excerpt reads, "There are those who believe Black people possess the secret of joy and that it is this that will sustain them through any spiritual or moral or physical devastation." The incredulity inherent in Ricciardi's memoir is shared by Walker and guides her construction of Tashi, who emerges at the novel's end spiritually intact, despite the "physical devastation" of her circumcision. Further, it is her "cunning" that permits her to return to Olinka and, without suspicion, gain access to and kill M'Lissa.

5. Fischer does not suppose that ethnicity is created by individuals; instead, he suggests that individuals have the power to influence, and alter, collective understandings of what it means to have an ethnicity. Hence, ethnicity can undergo successive redefinitions. The call for a switch from "Black" to "African American" represents such an altering call. Dr. Ramona Edelin, later echoed by Reverend Jesse Jackson, called for an identity name that recognizes the cultural and geographical origin of the peoples once called Black. Correspondingly, "African American" became the name of choice for many in the population. See Smitherman's "'What Is Africa to Me?': Language, Ideology and 'African American'" for a historical overview of ethnic identity naming and the ideological consequences.

6. Walker's interrogation of her relationship to Africa really begins with her first volume of poetry, *Once,* and "Karamojans," a poem about an African population "Never civilized" (23). The poem describes an idyllic Africa represented by "A tall man / Without clothes / Beautiful / Like a statue" (20). But later, this beauty is contradicted once we get "close up" and see that "His eyes / Are running / Sores" (21). Walker describes the beautiful man as "The Noble Savage" and describes the women in terms of their bodies: "Bare breasts loose / In the Sun / The skin Cracked / The nipples covered / With flies" (22). Her description here is heavily reminiscent of Conrad's "dark woman" roaming freely in "the heart of darkness." As well, this *National Geographic*–like depiction further demonstrates Walker's indebtedness to the Western anthropological tradition.

7. I have selected *Meridian* because, though *The Third Life of Grange Copeland* is as much about women as it is about Grange, the women are only discussed in relation to him. Barbara Christian discusses the development of Alice Walker's writing from *The Third Life of Grange Copeland* to *Meridian* in "Novels for Everyday Use: The Novels of Alice Walker." There, she focuses on Grange's lives and Ruth's in contrast to *Meridian*'s focus on self-discovery. Christian suggests that these novels show Walker's change in focus from private experiences to community maintenance. It is this focus in *Meridian* that guided my choice to compare it with Tashi's story in *Possessing.* I focus my discussion by tracing a line from Walker's first novel named for a woman, centering on her growth in

relation to men and community, to *Possessing*, which does the same but from an expanded cultural vantage point.

8. For an extended example of quilting as a metaphor for fiction, see Whitney Otto's *How to Make an American Quilt: A Novel*. Also, see Houston A. Baker and Charlotte Pierce Baker, "Patches: Quilts and Community in Alice Walker's 'Everyday Use,'" *Southern Review* 21 (1985): 706–20. Baker and Baker discuss the quiltmaker as a woman novelist who uses bits and pieces from her life on the margins as material for her art. Also, they discuss the quilt as loss and potential, an emblem of difference, a crafting of identity that joins people into one group while separating them from other groups, or collectives, of people.

9. I echo McDowell's point that Meridian is also an extension of the tree (275). Additionally, note that Walker's foremother Hurston opens her story of Janie Starks with a tree metaphor: "Janie saw her life like a great tree in leaf with the things suffered, things enjoyed, things done and undone" (*Their Eyes* 20). See "Zora Neale Hurston and the Speakerly Text" in Gates, *Signifying Monkey*, 170–217. This metaphor as grounding for Walker's first female protagonist is symbolic of her recognition of her indebtedness to Southern slave history and culture as well as to Hurston's literary precedence. Again, see "Looking for Zora" (Walker 1979). *Possessing* is prefaced by reference to a bumper sticker that reads: "When the axe came into the forest, the tree said the handle is one of us." Taken together, these references indicate Walker's use of genealogy and kinship, embodied in the family tree, as a creative impulse and design.

10. Rachel Stein, in her "Returning to the Sacred Tree," offers a reading of *Meridian* that parallels mine here. Stein, however, emphasizes Walker's rediscovery of Hurston and reads the novel as Walker's return to "Hurston's writing about black women, nature and indigenous culture" (86). Nonetheless, her sense of return—"a dual movement that travels backward to reclaim previous texts and history and that also, simultaneously, veers forward, turning what has been reclaimed in a new direction" (85)—mirrors my sankofa frame. Stein also examines the tree as a means for Walker to revisit Hurston's examination of Native American cultures, for the tree is a parallel natural image to the Sacred Serpent Indian Mound that grows on Meridian's family farm. As such, Walker links African and Native American peoples, a critical linking for her *By the Light of My Father's Smile*, wherein she creates the Mundo, a half-African and half-Indian people.

11. Though this is not explicitly stated or argued in Holloway's *Moorings and Metaphors*, it is my sense that she uses race as a means of representing what Marable has identified as Blackness.

12. For a detailed discussion of Walker's envisioning of her relationship to this foremother of Black American women's literature, see her "Looking for Zora." See also Marjorie Pryse's "Zora Neale Hurston, Alice Walker, and the Ancient Power of Black Women," in Pryse and Spillers (1–24).

13. For a discussion of Zora Neale Hurston's use of folklore in her fiction, see Howard J. Faulkner, "*Mules and Men*": Fiction as Folklore."

14. I cannot help but be struck by the alliterative parallel in the names of the ancestral characters Miss Lissie and M'Lissa. It is as if Walker constructs an ancestor who impresses the importance of engaging history and confronting its challenges, then progresses to create an ancestor who offers a tradition that is accepted unchallenged. Through the lineage of these two women, Walker's fiction illustrates the importance of embracing history

and indigenous traditions simultaneously with our analysis of these traditions within our present circumstances. As she says, her objective is not to "second the masses' motions, whatever they are," but "to explore or to challenge" the motions provided for her (qtd. in O'Brien 340).

15. For a discussion of representations of female circumcision in fiction, see Linda McNeeley Strong-Leek's *Excising the Spiritual, Physical and Psychological Self.*

16. In *Possessing,* Evelyn-Tashi also refers to her own "bathing." She questions M'Lissa as to why it is that "it is a woman's vulva that is destroyed? 'Bathed,' as they say, 'cleaned off'" (246).

17. Set on the campus of the University of Calabar, *Double Yoke* focuses on the lives and experiences of educated women. The novel's female protagonist, Nko, during a frank discussion with her mates about sex, comments that white "women are not clitorised . . . awful" (157; ellipsis dots in original). This problematic observation is compounded by the single response, "[w]ell, different people, different customs" (157). Emecheta allows this opportune moment to critique the ritual to pass. Katherine Fishburn discusses this silence as especially troubling given Emecheta's feminism (147–52).

18. I say "quasi-religious," because such folk belief is not supported by a search of scripture. Although it is taught that circumcision is ordered by Islam, and one form of ritual female circumcision is called *sunna,* which means "sanctioned by the prophet," there are no references to it in the *Holy Qur'an* as a requirement for women (Williams-Moen 5). Through personal communication, Elam Muhammad, Imam at Masjid Wali Mahmoud in Lansing, Michigan, informs me that the *Qur'an* does not sanction circumcision and hence "to refer to it as [any form of] *sunna* is misleading."

19. See the introduction to Gay Wilentz's *Binding Cultures,* wherein she offers a detailed discussion of women as maintainers and transmitters of cultural knowledge and practices, and suggests that such transmission is exclusively women's domain (xix).

20. Though the cultural "justifications" are presented in the novel through various character voices, Walker uses Bakhtinian hybrid constructions to undermine these representations. I discuss some of these instances more directly below. For discussions of Walker's use of multiple voice narration, see Stephen Souris's "Multipleperspectival Consensus."

21. For a similar criticism, see Margaret Kent Bass's "Alice's Secret," where she not only argues that Walker asserts a kinship tie with Tashi, but also that Walker attempts to use that bond as a defense against claims of imperialism. Bass writes: "[N]either Walker's African heritage nor her First World benevolence protects her from the charge of cultural condescension, and I would suggest that her race and gender, and the establishment of a family tie lend not only tremendous power to Walker's words but also a misleading authority and authenticity to her narrative" (4). She further suggests that Walker's narrative is bereft with a "smugness that allows Walker to justify her own imperialistic impulse by explaining that some distant relative of hers was probably mutilated" (9). These observations by Bass parallel my earlier reading of Walker in "Postmodern Ethnography and the Womanist Mission: Postcolonial Sensibilities in *Possessing the Secret of Joy*" *African American Review* 30, no. 2 (1996): 237–43.

22. I make this comparison based on the argument that women who have been circumcised do not experience pleasure from sex because it is too painful, yet men, who prefer the smaller openings, find circumcised women sexually pleasing. See, for example, Olayinka Koso-Thomas's *The Circumcision of Women: A Strategy for Eradication.* Also,

Walker makes this point in the novel: Tashi tell us that sex, after her circumcision, "was very hard" because she had been sewn so tight, and M'Lissa retorts "the men like it tight" (245). Tashi then confesses that she has never received pleasure from sex (246).

Also, the image of the mummy woman in *Meridian* is brought about by one of the parables that informs Tashi's understanding of her "Life Like Condition." Pierre relays the story of Torabe and his promiscuous wife, whose body was "dragged from the river and left to rot, her body food for vultures and rodents" (139). Marilene O'Shay was thrown into the Great Salt Lake by her husband because "she was so generous with sharing herself," and she resurfaces in the circus preyed upon by vulturous spectators (9).

Notes to Chapter 3

1. See Barnes; Cliff especially notes this intersection in *No Telephone to Heaven,* as I will later discuss, and in the title story from the collection *The Store of a Million Items.*

2. Here, when I use the term *racial,* I have chosen to place it in quotation marks because Cliff plays with the notion of race in popular thought. She does not specify Clare as black or white, but gives a history of the intersections of black and white in Clare's ancestry. This ambiguity of "racial" placement is a key issue for Cliff, and she infuses into this ambiguity a power and a dis-ease. That is, to be unraced is equally as problematic as being "raced." For further commentary on Cliff's play with issues of race, see Judith Raiskin's chapter "With the 'Logic of a Creole,'" in her *Snow on the Cane Fields.* As well, see Lindsay Pentolfe Aegerter's "Michelle Cliff and the Paradox of Privilege," *College English* 59, no. 8 (1997): 898–915, where she examines Cliff's representation of racial and class alliances.

3. This phrase is generally understood in terms of continental African literature. I use it here, though, because it refers to literature that, according to Abiola Irele, evidences a "pronounced social consciousness" where the writers "direct their attention mainly to the broader social and political aspects of the conflicts that arise as a result of colonialism" (154). This literature is also marked by a focus on alienation, exile, and the external conditioning of characters rather than on their inner responses. It is the focus on "external conditions" that grounds Jameson's and Harlow's analyses, and forms Cliff's point of divergence.

4. Jameson argues that while third-world literature purports to be "private and invested with a properly political dimension in the form of national allegory[,] the story of the private individual destiny is always an allegory of the embattled situation of the public third-world culture and society" (69). Though his use of "third-world" is problematic here, his remarks suggest a nonessentializing acknowledgment that not all such texts are political, but when there are politics, all politics are national allegory. I make use of this qualification in my analysis of Cliff, and I see it as useful to the previous discussion of Walker, as well. Nonetheless, for critiques of Jameson's use of "third-world" and the issues such usage raises for reader positionality, see Aijaz Ahmad, Homi Bhabha, and S. P. Mohanty.

5. See also Stephen Slemon's "Post Colonial Allegory and the Transformation of History."

6. Cliff also wrote an article where she discusses the need to recover and bring to attention the work of black women artists. The references to these artists here can be seen as her attempt to do so.

7. Both regions were under British colonial control, composed of heterogeneous populations separated during the colonial period via administrative policies, and in both cases

European-designed education partially integrated individual members of the indigenous population into the colonial political and economic structure. In both regions education acted as a programmed alienation process.

8. This is symbolic of the way Beloved in Morrison's *Beloved* is a representation of both historical remembering and dismembering. See my "Hearing, Reading, and Being Read by Beloved," *NWSAJ* 10, no. 2 (1998): 13–31.

9. "Shuffle Along" by Eubie Blake and Noble Sissle is a well-known Harlem Renaissance musical revue. Its 1921 opening on Broadway marked the beginning of interest in black music production. That Cliff uses this specific musical is telling in that it connects her protagonist, culturally and socially, to black America. In *Abeng* we have a Jamaican schoolteacher announcing that not only is Zora Neale Hurston an influence on him, but that the writings of the Harlem Renaissance is a must for his schoolchildren's reading. Significantly, "Shuffle Along" garnered much acclaim because it reinforced negative images of black people, and it made a space for other "formulaic hybrids of blacked up comedians, mammy songs, and darky skits [that] were a scant beyond minstrel shows" (Watson 106). Josephine Baker was relegated to a chorus line position in the production, for she was "small, skinny and unacceptably dark" (Watson 110). The issue of color as it plays itself out in American and Jamaican relationships seems key to Cliff's inquiry into a diaspora sistered kinship. Cliff's choice of "Shuffle Along" also emphasizes her focus on the function of color in black kinship relationships.

10. In contrast to my reading, Carole Boyce Davies argues that while Kitty romanticizes and "deals emotively with African identification," she does not fully embrace it ("Writing Home" 69).

11. Interestingly, when these characters are not women they are gay men. For example, in *No Telephone,* Clare's journey to self is paralleled and accompanied by the presence of Harry/Harriet. Although I discuss the sexual dynamics of their relationship in chapter 5 below, for analysis of Harry/Harriet in this context see Sethuraman's "Evidence-Cum-Witness," 273–75.

12. In contrast, the sign on the truck in which Clare rides is painted red and yellow. The red here recalls her connection to her mother and other red people, while the yellow encodes those who are morphologically indistinct, not white, not red, not brown, but some pale yet tinted hue.

13. Here Cliff intersects with Paule Marshall's *Brown Girl, Brownstones.* Marshall's novel engages the first wave of Caribbean migration and examines the conflicts that arise as these new immigrants construct a sense of their homeland in their new home, New York City.

14. An important parallel is found in Jamaica Kincaid's *Annie John* and its sequel, *Lucy,* which together chronicle a young girl's growth in a *bildungsroman* style similar to that of Cliff's *Abeng* and *No Telephone to Heaven.* Set in Antigua, Annie John's trek to adolescence is fraught with identity crises, minus the issue of color. For a reading of Kincaid's novel through a frame similar to my reading of Cliff, see Rosemary George's *The Politics of Home* (New York: Cambridge, 1996), 173–74.

15. A pattern of such casting can be found in other Caribbean writings. Though Boy inhibits Clare's indulging sankofa anxieties, in other fictions, characters who attempt a return to their roots, like the title character in Andrew Salkey's *The Late Emancipation of Jerry Stover,* find the result disastrous. Also, John Stewart's *Last Cool Days* confronts the issue of color and identity with a starkness prophetic of Cliff. Stewart, like Cliff, has had

long residence in the United States. Like Trumper in George Lamming's *In the Castle of My Skin,* the Caribbean writer may necessarily have to leave home "to know what it mean to fin' race," to comprehend the complexities of identity so profoundly encoded in his or her homeland.

16. In 1946, R. W. Thompson published his *Black Caribbean,* which contains a section on Jamaica entitled "The Land of Look Behind." There he describes the interior of Jamaica and the politics of the nation's/island's interior beauty. The descriptions of this space as exotic and free manifest themselves in the history of geographical exploitation, which has cast Jamaica as a paradise for wealthy vacationers. In her short story collection *Mint Tea,* Christine Craig also engages this imaging and its effects on the land and its people.

Notes to Chapter 4

1. This is a play on Aidoo's title as well as on the expressions "going through changes" and "put through changes," from the African American linguistic community. Clarence Major, in his historical dictionary *Juba to Jive* (New York: Penguin, 1994), defines the first phrase as "experiencing emotional or psychological problems," and the latter as "to make a person uncomfortable by doing or saying something that contradicts with their version of reality" (86). Likewise, Smitherman defines the first phrase as having "problems in one's personal life; unanticipated emotional experiences" (*Black Talk* 76–77). Aptly, we witness Aidoo's Esi going through and being put through "changes."

2. See my "Slavery in the Diaspora Consciousness: Ama Ata Aidoo's Conversations," wherein I discuss the influence of Nkrumahan politics on Aidoo's writing.

3. For me, at this analytical moment, these authors are both readers of texts and writers. It is crucial to the success of my work that I convey the importance of seeing the writer as a reader—Alice Walker is a reader of an African text—and the reader as writer. Likewise, scholars and critics represent an Africa in the texts they produce to explicate literary texts they have encountered. At times, I realize the reader may find this flip-flopping of positions unnerving. But I think it shows the fluidity of the boundaries between readers/writers and critics/writers.

4. It is only fair to acknowledge that in an author's note to *Changes* Aidoo writes: "[t]o the reader, a confession and to the critic, an apology . . . [*Changes*] is not meant to contribute to any debate however current." As with Alice Walker's readers' directive, although I take note of this disclaimer, I find it too restrictive.

5. Vincent Odamtten astutely argues that the historical contextualization is "a specific piece of Ghana's colonial past," and chooses the backdrop of rising British colonialism in Fantiland as the point of departure for his discussion. See his chapter on *Anowa.*

6. Thomas Echewa and John A. Williams debated these points in *Negro Digest,* and like Aidoo, Echewa asserts that African Americans and continental Africans are cousins. However, where he insists that the kinship is limited by this distant relation, Aidoo draws consistent parallels that close the gap.

7. This play also intersects with Angelou's representations of her own life in Ghana, in *All of God's Children Need Travelling Shoes.* Adell discusses this novel within the frame of double consciousness and offers insights that make my parallel clear. See her chapter 5.

8. In his *The African Novel in English* (119–32), M. Keith Booker offers a reading of

Killjoy that situates the novel with Nkrumahan Ghanaian politics, and which at times intersects with my reading.

9. I mark this interest with the publication of several seminal studies, namely the 1981 publication of Lloyd Brown's *Women Writers in Black Africa* and the 1985 Black Women Writers and the Diaspora Conference, followed by the 1986 publication of *Ngambika: Studies of Women in African Literature* (eds. Davies and Graves) and the 1987 special issue of *African Literature Today* (eds. Jones, Palmer, and Jones) dedicated to discussions of women's texts.

10. New Orleans, the city of mixture, is the subject of several poems in *Someone Talking to Sometime*. Related to my focus on language here, though, one of the poems about New Orleans, "The City—An Apology to Patricia," marks the cultural syncretism of New Orleans with a line that uses linguistic phrases from the various populations—"this city was parleyed depuis / longtemps"—alongside the regionalism that indicates New Orleans's geographical and diasporic location—"pickaninnies pour the hot sauce"; "big House"; and all along "the brown waters of the / Mississippi" (41, 42). In her "Ama Ata Aidoo and the African Diaspora," Hill-Lubin offers a parallel reading of this poem and others.

11. Elsewhere, I have argued that these contemplations reflect a Reading of, or signifyin' on, Western constructions of African women as victims of patriarchy who are unable, or unwilling, to resist these traditions. In this line, Aidoo challenges not only the tradition and the claims of African women's inability to do so, but also the presumption that sexist oppression is a traditional African tradition. See my "Colored Readings." In *Reading Sites: Social Difference and Reader Response*, eds. P. Schweickart and E. Flynn (New York: MLA, 2003).

12. See also Carole Boyce Davies's "Maidens, Mistresses and Matrons: Feminine Images in Selected Soyinka Works," *Ngambika*, 75–88. Davies offers a discussion of this characterization of women in men's fiction, and particularly in Wole Soyinka's dramas.

13. See also McWilliams's discussion where she contrasts Esi and best friend Opokuya's free articulations with Fusena silences, especially pp. 352–53.

14. The issue of the rings raises the question of the degree to which traditions can be dishonored. Ali professes that he is Moslem, and so is Fusena. Esi desires to abide by the tenets of Islam in the polygamous endeavor. Specifically, then, *the Qur'an* instructs the man considering taking another wife that "[i]f [you] cannot do justice, [then] marry only one or that which your right hand possesses . . . if [he] cannot treat them with perfect equality in material things as in love and affection, then marry only one" (*The Qur'an*, S4:127). Ali obviously sees Esi's wearing his ring as "equality in material things," while Esi sees this as an injustice to Fusena.

Notes to Chapter 5

1. This is a direct reference to Ishmael Reed's collection of critical essays *Writin' Is Fightin': Thirty-Seven Years of Boxing on Paper* (New York: Atheneum, 1988). In these essays, Reed exposes the degree to which black writing is a revolutionary act of resistance.

2. Indeed, Collins attached this to an analysis of Walker's concept of womanism, focusing on the part of the definition she claims, and rightly so, is overlooked by black women claiming to be, in fact, womanists; according to the excerpt, a womanist is "a woman who loves other women sexually and/or nonsexually" (Collins 65; Walker, *Search* xi).

3. Additionally, bell hooks in her "Writing the Subject" argues a position in concert with Hoogland's. Hooks posits that Celie and Shug's sexual relationship leaves heterosexual bonds unthreatened and likewise does not "affirm the possibility that women can be fulfilled in a life that does not include intimate relationships with men" (457). Like Hoogland, hooks critiques Walker's narrative for the way in which she "makes the powerful suggestion that sexual desire can disrupt and subvert oppressive structures," yet "this realization is undermined by the refusal to acknowledge it as threatening—dangerous" (456).

4. In fact, when Mr. comes requesting Nettie's hand in marriage and is told he can only have Celie, Pa takes away her culturally prescribed properties of womanness. Describing her as "ugly," he informs Mr. that Celie "ain't fresh though, . . . spoiled. Twice" (17).

5. In naming Celie "lady," I recall the vernacular tradition that identifies aged and premarital (without children) females not as women, but as young ladies and older ladies. In this context, then, "lady" indicates a female's status as not yet woman, while the title "woman" is left for those who have entered heterosexual contracts.

6. Interestingly, Celie describes Shug to Nettie as "a beautiful something . . . look like a big rose" (167). This link between Shug and her vagina highlights the centrality of their love relationship to her discovery of herself and her voice.

7. I should note that in the essay I excerpt, hooks indicates that as a child, in contrast to Walker, she remembers the active presence of male homosexuals, but she also recalls acrimonious conversations about lesbians as a "specifically insidious threat to the continuation of black families," because womanness, morally and religiously, was grounded in "child-bearing," making lesbianism "unnatural" ("Homophobia in Black Communities" 123, 121).

8. The association of purple with royalty and Christianity is traced back to Christ's trial before crucifixion. Not only is He crowned "King of the Jews," but He is also given a purple vestment to mark that royal status; see Matthew 21:27–31. In Christian liturgy, purple symbolizes penitence and sorrow and is worn by clergy throughout the Lenten and Advent seasons. See George Ferguson's *Signs and Symbols in Christian Art,* 152. Here, I read Walker as appropriating this symbolism to indicate the need for societal penance for using the Bible—and God—to support homophobia and perpetuate systems that restrict women's freedoms.

9. In her *Bodies That Matter,* Judith Butler discusses these ideas about male and female homosexuality (124–27).

10. In *No Telephone to Heaven,* Clare peruses a tattered copy of *Jane Eyre.* While reading the passage where Jane promises her mother to flee, Clare imagines first that she is Jane, "betrayed. Left to wander. Solitary. Motherless" (116). But later, Clare reasons that she could not be Jane, "small and pale. English," but that she was instead the "wild-maned Bertha . . . Captive. Ragôut. Mixture. Confused. Jamaican . . . All Bertha. All Clare" (116).

11. As I have already said, Cliff's poem "The Laughing Mulatto" makes the notion of racial malleability clear. Suzanne Bost, for example, goes further than I to quite convincingly argue that Cliff's writings can be read as within the African American literary tradition of the "tragic mulatta." See her "Fluidity Without Postmodernism."

12. In an interview with Meryl Schwartz, Cliff suggests that Zoe embarks on the hunt in response to reading about the rape of a young girl, and the hunt symbolizes Clare's "tak-

ing power as a girl" but "through a male mode," for "the power she's witnessed is always through a male mode" (602). This reinforces my claims about Clare's male identification and highlights her exclusion from female domains, as well. On the female exclusion, Cliff notes that Clare's "access to female power is embodied in the person of her grandmother," who "shuns" her after she kills the bull (603).

13. In her interview with Meryl Schwartz, Cliff suggests that the novel does not inform us of Harriet's fate, that in fact she lives on, which makes my claim here problematic. However, the ambiguity of the novel and the implications of Clare's homosexual desires in *No Telephone to Heaven* sustain my reading.

14. In discussing the "overtly sexual theme" of her latest novel, which I discuss below, Walker says that "sexuality is the place where life has fallen into a pit for women," and women must begin to write "more truthfully about the profound mystery of sex" (E. White 45). This mystery is aptly captured in the imagery of this scene.

15. I refer to Wilentz's discussion in "The Politics of Exile," wherein she claims that Aidoo casts Sissie's response to "this attempt at a lesbian relationship as a perversion of woman love and part of the degeneration of European family life" (84).

references

Abbandonato, Linda. "A View from 'Elsewhere': Subversive Sexuality and the Rewriting of the Heroine's Story in *The Color Purple*." *PMLA* (1991): 1106–15.

Abrahams, Roger. *African Folktales*. New York: Pantheon Books, 1983.

Achebe, Chinua. "The Song of Ourselves." *New Statesman and Society* 3, no. 8 (1990): 30–32.

Adell, Sandra. *Double Consciousness/Double Bind: Theoretical Issues in Twentieth-Century African American Literature*. Urbana: University of Illinois Press, 1994.

Aidoo, Ama Ata. *Anowa*. London: Longman, 1970.

———. *Changes: A Love Story*. London: Women's Press, 1991.

———. *Dilemma of a Ghost*. London: Longman, 1965.

———. "Ghana: To Be a Woman." In *Sisterhood Is Global*. Ed. Robin Morgan. New York: Doubleday, 1984. 258–65.

———. *No Sweetness Here*. London: Longman, 1970.

———. *Our Sister Killjoy: Or Reflections from a Black-eyed Squint*. London: Longman, 1966.

———. *Someone Talking to Sometime*. Harare: College Press, 1985.

———. "'That Capacious Topic': Gender Politics." In *Critical Fictions: The Politics of Imaginative Writing*. Ed. Philomena Mariani. Seattle: Bay Press, 1991. 151–54.

———. "Unwelcome Pals and Decorative Slaves: The Woman Writer, the Woman as a Writer in Modern Africa." *Afa* I (1982): 34–43.

Aijaz, Ahmad. "Jameson's Rhetoric of Otherness and the 'National Allegory.'" *Social Text* 17 (Fall 1987): 3–25.

Alcoff, Linda. "The Problem of Speaking for Others." *Cultural Critique* 20 (1991): 5–32.

"Alice Walker's Appeal." *Essence* JL (1992): 102.

Angelou, Maya. *All God's Children Need Travelling Shoes*. New York: Vintage, 1976.

Appiah, Kwame Anthony. *In My Father's House*. London: Methuen, 1992.

Armah, Ayi Kwei. *Fragments*. Boston: Houghton Mifflin, 1970.

———. *Two Thousand Seasons*. London: Heinemann, 1979.

Asante, Molefi Kete. "Putting Africa at the Center." *Newsweek* (23 September 1991): 46.

Azodo, Ada Uzoamaka. "Facing the Millennium: An Interview with Ama Ata Aidoo." In *Emerging Perspectives on Ama Ata Aidoo*. Eds. Ada U. Azodo and Gay Wilentz. Trenton, N.J.: Africa World Press, 1999. 429–41.

Azodo, Ada U., and Gay Wilentz, eds. *Emerging Perspectives on Ama Ata Aidoo.* Trenton, N.J.: Africa World Press, 1999.

Bâ, Mariama. *So Long a Letter.* Portsmouth, N.H.: Heinemann, 1989.

Bakhtin, Mikhail M. *The Dialogic Imagination.* Trans. Caryl Emerson and Michael Holquist. Ed. Michael Holquist. Austin: University of Texas Press, 1981.

Barnes, Fiona R. "Resisting Cultural Cannibalism: Oppositional Narratives in Michelle Cliff's *No Telephone to Heaven.*" *Journal of Midwest Modern Language Association* 25, no. 1 (1992): 23–31.

Bass, Margaret. "Alice's Secret." *CLA Journal* 38, no. 1 (1994): 1–11.

Bell, Roseanne P. "The Absence of the African Woman Writer." *CLA Journal* 21, no. 4 (1978): 491–98.

Berghan, Marion. *Images of Africa in Black American Literature.* Totowa, N.J.: Bowman, 1977.

Berrian, Brenda. "The Afro-American–West African Marriage Question: Its Literary and Historical Context." In *Women in African Literature Today.* Eds. E. D. Jones, E. Palmer, and M. Jones. Spec. issue of *African Literature Today* 15 (1987): 152–59.

Bhabha, Homi. "In a Spirit of Calm Violence." In *After Colonialism: Imperial Histories and Postcolonial Displacements.* Ed. Gyan Prakash. Princeton, N.J.: Princeton University Press, 1995. 326–43.

Bjornson, Richard, ed. *Critical Theory and African Literature.* Spec. issue of *Research in African Literatures* 21, no. 1 (1990): 5–175.

Booker, M. Keith. *The African Novel in English: An Introduction.* Portsmouth, N.H.: Heinemann, 1998.

Bost, Suzanne. "Fluidity Without Postmodernism: Michelle Cliff and the 'Tragic Mulatta' Tradition." *African American Review* 32, no. 4 (1998): 673–89.

Braendlin, Bonnie. "Alice Walker's *The Temple of My Familiar* as Pastiche." *American Literature* 68 (1996): 47–67.

Brathwaite, E. K. *Contradictory Omens: Cultural Diversity and Integration in the Caribbean.* Jamaica: Savacou, 1974.

Brown, Lloyd. *Woman Writers in Black Africa.* Westport, Conn.: Greenwood Press, 1981.

Brown, W. J., M.P. *The Land of Look Behind.* London: Latima, 1949.

Busia, Abena. "Words Whispered over the Voids: A Context for Black Women's Rebellious Voices in the Novel of the African Diaspora." In *Black Feminist Criticism and Critical Theory.* Vol. 3 of *Studies in Black American Literature.* Eds. Houston A. Baker and Joe Weixlmann. Greenwood, Fla.: Penkewill, 1988. 1–41.

Butler, Judith. *Bodies That Matter: On the Discursive Limits of Sex.* New York: Routledge, 1993.

———. *Gender Trouble: Feminism and the Subversion of Identity.* New York: Routledge, 1990.

Campbell, Mavis. *The Maroon of Jamaica, 1655–1796.* Trenton, N.J.: Africa World Press, 1990.

Carby, Hazel. *Race Men.* Cambridge, Mass.: Harvard University Press, 1998.

———. *Reconstructing Womanhood: The Emergence of the Afro-American Woman Novelist.* New York: Oxford University Press, 1987.

Cheney Coker, Syl. *The Last Harmattan of Alusine Dunbar.* Portsmouth, N.H.: Heinemann, 1990.

Chodorow, Nancy. *The Reproduction of Mothering: Psychoanalysis and the Sociology of Gender.* Berkeley: University of California Press, 1978.

Christian, Barbara. "An Angle of Seeing: Motherhood in Buchi Emecheta's *Joys of Motherhood* and Alice Walker's *Meridian.*" In *Black Feminist Criticism.* New York: Pergamon, 1985. 211–52.

———. "Black Woman Artist as Wayward." In *Black Woman Writers (1950–1980): A Critical Evaluation.* Ed. Mari Evans. Garden City, N.J.: Anchor, 1984. 457–77.

———. "The Race for Theory." In *Within the Circle: An Anthology of African American Literary Criticism from the Harlem Renaissance to the Present.* Ed. Angelyn Mitchell. Durham, N.C.: Duke University Press, 1994. 348–59.

Clark, VèVè. "Developing Diaspora Literacy and Marasa Consciousness." In *Comparative American Identities: Race, Sex and Nationality in the Modern Text.* Ed. Hortense Spillers. New York: Routledge, 1991. 40–61.

Cliff, Michelle. *Abeng.* New York: Penguin, 1985.

———. *Bodies of Water.* New York: Dutton, 1990.

———. *Claiming an Identity They Taught Me to Despise.* Watertown, Mass.: Persephone Press, 1980.

———. "Clare Savage as a Crossroads Character." In *Caribbean Women Writers: Essays from the First International Conference.* Ed. Selwyn Cudjoe. Wellesley, Mass.: Calaloux, 1990. 263–68.

———. *Free Enterprise.* New York: Dutton, 1993.

———. *The Land of Look Behind.* New York: Firebrand, 1985.

———. *No Telephone to Heaven.* New York: Dutton, 1987.

———. *The Store of a Million Items.* New York: Mariner, 1998.

Cohen, Arthur P. "Culture as Identity: An Anthropologist's View." *New Literary History* 24 (1993): 195–209.

Collins, Patricia Hill. *Fighting Words: Black Women and the Search for Justice.* Minneapolis: University of Minnesota Press, 1998.

Craig, Christine. *Mint Tea and Other Stories.* Portsmouth, N.H.: Heinemann, 1993.

Cullen, Countee. "Heritage." In *Color.* New York: Harper, 1925. Reprinted in *The New Negro: Voices of the Harlem Renaissance.* Ed. Alain Locke. New York: Macmillan, 1992. 250–53.

Culler, Jonathan. *On Deconstruction: Theory and Criticism after Structuralism.* Ithaca, N.Y.: Cornell University Press, 1982.

Davies, Carole Boyce. *Black Women, Writing and Identity: Migrations of the Subject.* New York: Routledge, 1994.

———. "Writing Home: Gender and Heritage in the Works of Afro-Caribbean/American Women Writers." In *Out of the Kumbla: Caribbean Woman and Literature.* Eds. Carole Boyce Davies and Elaine Savory Fido. Trenton, N.J.: Africa World Press, 1990. 59–73.

Davies, Carole B., and Anne A. Graves, eds. *Ngambika: Studies of Women in African Literature.* Trenton, N.J.: Africa World Press, 1986.

de Lauretis, Teresa. *Technologies of Gender: Essays on Theory, Film, and Fiction.* Bloomington: Indiana University Press, 1987.

Dent, Gina. "Black Pleasure, Black Joy: An Introduction." In *Black Popular Culture.* Ed. Gina Dent. Seattle: Bay Press, 1992. 1–20.

Dieke, Ikenna. "Toward a Monoastic Idealism: The Thematics of Alice Walker's *The Temple of My Familiar.*" *African American Review* 26, no. 4 (1992): 507–14.

Dorsinville, Max. "Senghor and the Song of Exile." In *Exile and Tradition: Studies in African and Caribbean Literature.* Ed. Rowland Smith. New York: Africana, 1976. 62–73.

Douglass, Frederick. "An Address to the Colored People of the United States (29 September 1848)." In *Negro Social and Political Thought, 1850–1920.* Ed. Howard Brotz. New York: Random House, 1966. 210.

Drachler, Jacob. *Black Homeland/Black Diaspora.* Port Washington, N.Y.: National University Press, 1975.

DuBois, W. E. B. "The Conservation of the Races." In *W. E. B. DuBois: A Reader.* Ed. Andrew Paschall. New York: Macmillan, 1971. 19–30.

———. "Pan-Africanism: A Mission in My Life." In *W. E. B. DuBois: A Reader.* Ed. Andrew Paschall. New York: Macmillan, 1971. 241–52.

———. *The Souls of Black Folk.* New York: A. C. McClurg, 1903. Reprint, New York: Viking, 1989.

DuPlessis, Rachel Blau. *Writing Beyond the Ending.* Bloomington: University of Indiana Press, 1985.

Echewa, Thomas O. "Africans vs Afro-Americans." *Negro Digest* (January 1965): 12–14.

———. "Reply to a Negro." *Negro Digest* (September 1965): 23–27.

Eichman, Erich. "The Cutting Edge." *National Review* 44 (1992): 48–49.

Eke, Maureen. "Diasporic Ruptures and (Re)membering History: Africa as Home and Exile in *Anowa* and *Dilemma of a Ghost.*" In *Emerging Perspectives on Ama Ata Aidoo.* Eds. Ada U. Azodo and Gay Wilentz. Trenton, N.J.: Africa World Press, 1999. 61–78.

El Dareer, Asma. *Woman, Why Do You Weep? Circumcision and Its Consequences.* London: Zed Press, 1982.

Emecheta, Buchi. *The Bride Price.* New York: Braziller, 1976.

———. *Our Own Freedom.* London: Sheba Feminist, 1981.

Esonwanne, Uzo. "'Race' and Hermeneutics: Paradigm Shift from Scientific to Hermeneutic Understanding of Race." *African American Review* 26 (1992): 565–82.

Faulkner, Howard J. "*Mules and Men*: Folklore as Fiction." *CLA Journal* 34 (1994): 331–39.

Ferguson, Ann. "Sex War: The Debate Between Radical and Libertarian Feminists." *Signs* 10, no. 1 (1984): 106–12.

Ferguson, George. *Signs and Symbols in Christian Art.* New York: Oxford, 1961.

Fields, Barbara J. "Ideology and Race in American History." In *Region, Race and Reconstruction: Essays in Honor of C. Vann Woodward.* Eds. J. Morgan Kousser and James M. McPherson. New York: Oxford University Press, 1982. 143–77.

———. "Slavery, Race and Ideology in the United States of America." *New Left Review* 181 (1990): 95–118.

Fischer, Michael M. "Ethnicity and the Post-Modern Arts of Memory." In *Writing Culture: The Poetics and Politics of Ethnography.* Eds. James Clifford and George Marcus. Berkeley: University of California Press, 1986. 194–233.

Fishburn, Katherine. *Reading Buchi Emecheta: Cross-Cultural Conversations.* Westport, Conn.: Greenwood Press, 1995.

Flax, Jane. "Signifying the Father's Desire: Lacan in a Feminist's Gaze." In *Criticism and Lacan: Essays and Dialogue on Language, Structure, and the Unconscious.* Eds. Patrick Colm Hogan and Lalita Pandit. Athens: University of Georgia Press, 1990. 109–19.

Foucault, Michel. *The Archaeology of Knowledge and the Discourse on Language.* Trans. Rupert Sawyer. New York: Pantheon, 1972. Originally published as *L'archéologie du savoir* (Paris: Éditions Gallimard, 1969).

———. "Film and Popular Memory: An Interview with Michel Foucault." *Radical Philosophy* 11 (1975): 24–29.

———. *Language, Counter-Memory, Practice: Selected Essays and Interviews.* Trans. Donald F. Bouchard and Sherry Simon. Ed. Donald Bouchard. Ithaca, N.Y.: Cornell University Press, 1977.

Frank, Katherine. "Women Without Men: The Feminist Novel in Africa." In *Women in African Literature Today.* Eds. E. D. Jones, E. Palmer, and M. Jones. Spec. issue of *African Literature Today* 15 (1987): 14–34.

Fruola, Christina. "The Daughter's Seduction: Sexual Violence and Literary History." *Signs* 11 (1986): 621–44.

Fuss, Diana. *Essentially Speaking: Feminism, Nature and Difference.* New York: Routledge, 1989.

Gadamer, Hans-Georg. *Truth and Method.* Trans. Joel Weinsheimer and Donald G. Marshall. New York: Crossroad, 1991. Originally published as *Warheit und Methode* (Tubingen: J. C. B. Mohr, 1960).

Garane, Jeanne. "History, Identity and the Constitution of the Female Subject: Maryse Condè's *Tituba.*" In *Black Women's Diaspora.* Vol. 2 of *Moving Beyond Boundaries.* Ed. C. B. Davies. New York: New York University Press, 1995. 153–64.

Garvey, Marcus, and Universal Negro Improvement Association Papers. Vol. 1. Berkeley: University of California Press, 1983.

Gates, Henry Louis. "Beware the New Pharaohs." *Newsweek* (23 September 1991): 47.

———. *Figures in Black: Words, Signs and the "Racial" Self.* New York: Oxford University Press, 1989.

———. *The Signifying Monkey: A Theory of African-American Literary Criticism.* New York: Oxford University Press, 1988.

Geertz, Clifford. "From the Native's Point of View: On the Nature of Anthropological Understanding." In *Interpretive Social Science: A Reader.* Ed. Paul Rabinow and William Sullivan. Berkeley: University of California Press, 1979. 225–41.

Gerima, Haile. "Spirit of the Dead." In *Jump Up and Say! A Collection of Black Storytelling.* Eds. Linda Goss and Clay Goss. New York: Simon and Schuster, 1995. 81–82.

Gikandi, Simon. "Narration at the Postcolonial Moment: History and Representation in *Abeng.*" In *Writing in Limbo: Modernism and Caribbean Literature.* Ithaca, N.Y.: Cornell University Press, 1992. 231–51.

Gilman, Sander L. *Inscribing the Other.* Lincoln: University of Nebraska Press, 1991.

Gilroy, Paul. *The Black Atlantic: Modernity and Double Consciousness.* Cambridge, Mass.: Harvard University Press, 1993.

———. "It's a Family Affair." In *Black Popular Culture.* Ed. Gina Dent. Seattle: Bay Press, 1992. 303–16.

Gourdine, Angeletta KM. "Slavery in the Diaspora Consciousness: Ama Ata Aidoo's *Conversations.*" In *Emerging Perspectives on Ama Ata Aidoo.* Eds. Ada Uzoamaka and Gay Wilentz. Trenton, N.J.: Africa World Press, 1999. 27–44.

Grandquist, Raoul, and John Stotesbury. *African Voices: Interviews with Thirteen African Writers*. Sydney, Australia: Dangaroo Press, 1989.

Grayson, Sandra. "Spirits of Asona Ancestors Come: Reading Asante Signs in Haile Gerima's *Sankofa*." *CLA Journal* (December 1998): 212–20.

Griffin, Susan. *Pornography and Silence: Culture's Revenge Against Nature*. New York: Harper and Row, 1983.

Haley, Alex. *Roots*. New York: Doubleday, 1986.

Harlow, Barbara. *Resistance Literature*. New York: Methuen, 1987.

Harris, Eddy. *Native Stranger: A Black American's Journey into the Heart of Africa*. New York: Random House, 1992.

Harris, Wilson. *Kas-Kas: Interviews with Three Caribbean Writers in Texas*. Arlington: University of Texas Press, 1972.

———. "Tradition and the West Indian Novel." In *The Tradition, the Writer, and Society: Critical Essays*. London: New Beacon, 1967. 28–47.

———. *The Womb of Space: The Cross-Cultural Imagination*. Westport, Conn.: Greenwood Press, 1983.

Henderson, Mae. "*The Color Purple:* Revisions and Redefinitions." *SAGE* 2 (1985): 14–18.

Hill-Lubin, Mildred A. "Ama Ata Aidoo and the African Diaspora." In *Emerging Perspectives on Ama Ata Aidoo*. Eds. Ada U. Azodo and Gay Wilentz. Trenton, N.J.: Africa World Press, 1999. 45–60.

Holloway, Karla. *Moorings and Metaphors: Figures of Culture and Gender in Black Women's Literature*. New Brunswick, N.J.: Rutgers University Press, 1992.

Hoogland, Renée. "Defining Differences: The Lavender Menace and *The Color Purple*." In *Lesbian Configurations*. New York: Columbia University Press, 1997. 11–23.

hooks, bell. "Choosing the Margin as a Space of Radical Openness." *Yearning: Race, Gender, and Cultural Politics*. Boston: South End Press, 1990. 145–53.

———. "Homophobia in Black Communities." *Talking Back: Thinking Feminist, Thinking Black*. Boston: South End Press, 1989. 120–26.

———. "The Oppositional Gaze: Black Female Spectators." *Black Looks: Race and Representation*. Boston: South End, 1992. 115–32.

———. "Writing the Subject: Reading the Color Purple." In *Reading Black, Reading Feminist: A Critical Anthology*. Ed. Henry Louis Gates, Jr. New York: Meridian, 1990. 454–70.

Hurston, Zora Neale. *Mules and Men*. Philadelphia: Lippencott, 1935; Bloomington: Indiana University Press, 1978.

———. *Tell My Horse*. Philadelphia: Lippencott, 1938; New York: Harper and Row, 1990.

———. *Their Eyes Were Watching God*. 1937 rpt. Urbana: University of Illinois Press, 1978.

Irele, Abiola. *African Experience in Literature and Ideology*. Exeter, N.H.: Heinemann, 1981.

Jahn, Janheinz. *History of Neo-African Literature: Writing in Two Continents*. Trans. Oliver Corbin and Ursula Lehrburger. London: Faber, 1968. Originally published as *Geschichte der neoafrikanischen Literatur* (Dusseldorf: Diederichs, 1966).

———. *Muntu: African Culture and the Western World*. New York: Grove Weidenfeld, 1990.

James, Adeola. *In Their Own Voices: African Women Writers Talk*. Portsmouth, N.H.: Heinemann, 1990.

Jameson, Frederic. "Postmodernism and Consumer Society." In *The Anti-Aesthetic: Essays on Postmodern Culture*. Ed. Hal Foster. Port Townsend, Wash.: Bay Press, 1983. 111–25.

———. "Third World Literature in the Era of Multinational Capitalism." *Social Text* 15 (Fall 1986): 65–88.

Johnson, Lemuel. "A-beng: (Re)Calling the Body in(to) Question." In *Out of the Kumbla: Caribbean Women and Literature*. Eds. Carole Boyce Davies and Elaine Savory Fido. Trenton, N.J.: Africa World Press, 1990. 112–42.

Jones, E. D., E. Palmer, and M. Jones, eds. *Women in African Literature Today*. Spec. issue of *African Literature Today* 15 (1987): 1–162.

Kaplan, Cora. *Seachanges: Culture and Feminism*. London: Verso, 1986.

Kenyatta, Jomo. *Facing Mt. Kenya*. London: Heinemann, 1965.

Killens, John. *Black Man's Burden*. New York: Trident, 1965.

———. "Brotherhood of Blackness." *Negro Digest* (May 1966): 4–10.

King, Bruce. *The New English Literatures: Cultural Nationalism in a Changing World*. New York: St. Martin's Press, 1980.

Korang, Kwaku Laribi. "Ama Ata Aidoo's Voyage Out: Mapping the Coordinates of Modernity and African Selfhood in *Our Sister Killjoy*." *Kunapipi* 14, no. 3 (1992): 50–61.

Koso-Thomas, Olayinka. *The Circumcision of Women: A Strategy for Eradication*. London: Zed, 1987.

Kourouma, Ahmadou. *The Suns of Independence*. Trans. Adrian Adams. New York: Africana, 1981. Originally published as *Les Soleils des indépendances* (London: Heinemann, 1968).

Kouyate, D'Jimo. "African Holocaust." *Michigan Citizen,* 2 October [waiting to hear from author], B8.

Lalla, Barbara. *Defining Jamaican Fiction: Marronage and the Discourse of Survival*. Tuscaloosa: University of Alabama Press, 1996.

Lamming, George. *In the Castle of My Skin*. London: Michael Joseph, 1953.

Lévi-Strauss, Claude. *The Elementary Structures of Kinship*. 2d ed. Trans. James Hurle Bell et al. Oxford: Beacon, 1969.

Lewis, Gordon K. *The Growth of the Modern West Indies*. London: MacGibbon and Kee, 1968.

Lightfoot-Klein, Hanny. "The Sexual Experience and Marital Adjustment of Genitally Circumcised and Infibulated Females in the Sudan." *The Journal of Sex Research* 26, no. 3 (1989): 375–92.

Lima, Maria. "Revolutionary Developments in Michelle Cliff's *No Telephone to Heaven* and Merle Collins' *Angel*." *ARIEL: A Review of International English Literature* 34, no. 1 (1983): 35–56.

Lindfors, Bernth. "The Image of the Afro-American in African Literature." *Association for Commonwealth Literature and Language Studies Bulletin* 4, no. 3 (1975): 19–26.

Major, Clarence. *Juba to Jive: A Dictionary of African American Slang*. New York: Viking, 1994.

Marable, Manning. "Race, Identity and Political Culture." In *Black Popular Culture*. Ed. Gina Dent. Seattle: Bay Press, 1992. 292–302.

Marshall, Paule. *Brown Girl, Brownstones*. New York: Westbury Press, 1981.

Mazrui, Ali. *Cultural Engineering and Nation Building in East Africa*. Evanston, Ill.: Northwestern University Press, 1972.

McDowell, Deborah. "The Self in Bloom: Alice Walker's *Meridian*." *CLA Journal* 24 (1981): 262–75.

McWilliams, Sally. "Strange as It May Seem: Feminism in Two Novels by Ama Ata Aidoo." In *Emerging Perspectives on Ama Ata Aidoo*. Eds. Ada U. Azodo and Gay Wilentz. Trenton, N.J.: Africa World Press, 1999. 333–62.

Mohanty, Satya P. "Us and Them: On the Philosophical Bases of Political Criticism." *Yale Journal of Criticism* 2, no. 2 (1989): 1–31.

Morrison, Toni. *Beloved*. New York: Random House, 1987.

———. "The Site of Memory." In *Out There: Marginalization and Contemporary Cultures*. Eds. Russell Ferguson, Martha Gever, Trinh T. Minh-ha, and Cornel West. Cambridge, Mass.: MIT Press, 1990. 299–305.

Mudimbe, V. Y. *Invention of Africa*. Bloomington: Indiana University Press, 1988.

Mullin, Michael. *Africa in America: Slave Acculturation and Resistance in the American South and the British Caribbean, 1736–1831*. Urbana: University of Illinois Press, 1994.

Nfah Abbenyi, Juliana M. "Flabberwhelmed or Turning History on Its Head? The Post Colonial Woman as Subject in Aidoo's *Changes: A Love Story*." In *Emerging Perspectives on Ama Ata Aidoo*. Eds. Ada U. Azodo and Gay Wilentz. Trenton, N.J.: Africa World Press, 1999. 281–302.

Ngugi wa Thiong'o. *Devil on the Cross*. London: Heinemann, 1982.

———. *The River Between*. London: Heinemann, 1965.

Nkrumah, Kwame. "Africa's Glorious Past." Address delivered at the opening of the First International Congress of Africanists, University of Ghana, Legon, 12 December 1962. Kwame Nkrumah Papers, Moorland-Spingarn Research Center, Howard University, Washington, D.C. 154–17:18.

———. *The Spectre of Black Power*. London: Panaf, 1968. Moorland-Spingarn Research Center, Howard University, Washington, D.C. Dabu Gizenga Collection on Kwame Nkrumah 128–5:83.

Nwapa, Flora. *Efuru*. Portsmouth, NH: Heinemann, 1966.

O'Brien, John. "Alice Walker: An Interview." *Alice Walker: Critical Perspectives Past and Present*. Eds. Henry Louis Gates, Jr., and K. A. Appiah. New York: Amistad Press, 1993. 326–46.

Odamtten, Vincent. *The Art of Ama Ata Aidoo: Polyectics and Reading Against Neocolonialism*. Gainesville: University Press of Florida, 1994.

Ogundipe-Leslie, Molara. "The Female Writer and Her Commitment." In *Women in African Literature Today*. Eds. E. D. Jones, E. Palmer, and M. Jones. Spec. issue of *African Literature Today* 15 (1987): 5–13.

Ogunyemi, Chikweyne Okonjo. "Womanism: The Dynamics of the Contemporary Black Female Novel in English." In *Revising the Word and the World*. Eds. VèVè Clark et al. Chicago: University of Chicago Press, 1993.

Okonkwo, Juliet. "The Talented Woman in African Literature." *African Quarterly* 15, no. 4 (1976): 36–47.

Olaniyan, Tejumola. "African American Critical Discourse and the Invention of Cultural Identities." *African American Review* 26, no. 4 (1992): 533–45.

Otto, Whitney. *How to Make an American Quilt: A Novel*. New York: Villard, 1991.

Outlaw, Lucius. "Toward a Critical Theory of 'Race.'" In *Anatomy of Racism*. Ed. David Theo Goldberg. Minneapolis: University of Minnesota Press, 1990. 58–82.

Patterson, Orlando. *The Children of Sisyphus*. London: New Authors, 1964.

Prince, Mary. "History of Mary Prince, A West Indian Slave, Restated By Herself." In *The Classic Narratives*. Ed. Henry Louis Gates, Jr. New York: New American Library, 1987.

Pryse, Marjorie, and Hortense Spillers. *Conjuring: Black Women, Fiction, and Literary Tradition*. Bloomington: Indiana University Press, 1985.

The Qur'an. Trans. Ali, Muhammad Mulanna. Islam, 1973.

Rabinow, Paul. "Representations Are Social Facts: Modernity and Post-Modernity in Anthropology." In *Writing Culture: The Poetics and Politics of Ethnography*. Eds. James Clifford and George Marcus. Berkeley: University of California Press, 1986. 234–61.

Raiskin, Judith. *Snow on the Cane Fields: Women's Writing and Creole Subjectivity*. Minneapolis: University of Minnesota Press, 1996.

Rian, Karen. "Sadomasochism and the Social Construction of Desire." In *Against Sadomasochism: A Radical Feminist Analysis*. Eds. Robin Linden, D. Ragano, D. Russell, and S. Star. Palo Alto, Calif.: Frog in the Well Press, 1982. 40–57.

Rich, Adrienne. "Compulsory Heterosexuality and Lesbian Representation." In *Women—Sex and Sexuality*. Eds. Catherine R. Stimpson and Ethel Spector Person. Chicago: University of Chicago Press, 1980. 62–91.

"Scarred for Life." *Day One*. ABC. WLAJ, Lansing. 20 September 1993. Journal Graphics Transcript no. 129.

Schwartz, Merle. "An Interview with Michelle Cliff." *Contemporary Literature* 34, no. 4 (1993): 595–619.

Sethuraman, Ramchandran. "Evidence-Cum-Witness: Subaltern, History, Violence, and the (De)Formation of Nation in Michelle Cliff's *No Telephone to Heaven*." *Modern Fiction Studies* 43, no. 1 (1997): 249–87.

Slemon, Stephen. "Monuments of Empire: Allegory/Counter-Discourse/Post Colonial Writing." *Kunapipi* 9, no. 3 (1987): 1–16.

———. "Post Colonial Allegory and the Transformation of History." *The Journal of Commonwealth Literature* 33, no. 1 (1988): 157–68.

Smitherman, Geneva. *Black Talk: Words from the Hood to the Amen Corner*. Boston: Houghton Mifflin, 1994.

———. "'What Is Africa to Me?': Language, Ideology and 'African American.'" *American Speech* 66, no. 3 (1991): 115–32.

Souris, Stephen. "Multiperspectival Consensus: Alice Walker's *Possessing the Secret of Joy*, the Multiple Narrator Novel and the Practice of 'Female Circumcision.'" *CLA Journal* 40, no. 4 (1997): 405–31.

Soyinka, Wole. *The Burden of Memory, the Muse of Forgiveness*. New York: Oxford, 1999.

———. *A Dance of the Forests*. London: Oxford University Press, 1963.

———. *The Interpreters*. London: Heinemann, 1970.

Spillers, Hortense. "Afterword: Cross-Currents, Discontinuities: Black Women's Fiction." In *Conjuring: Black Women's Fiction and Literary Tradition*. Eds. Marjorie Pryse and Hortense Spillers. Bloomington: Indiana University Press, 1985. 249–61.

Steady, Filomina C. "The Black Woman Cross-Culturally: An Overview." *The Black Woman Cross-Culturally*. Rochester, Vt.: Schenkman, 1981, 1985. 7–41.

Stein, Karen. "*Meridian*: Alice Walker's Critique of Revolution." *Black American Literature Forum* 20 (1986): 129–41.

Stein, Rachel. "Returning to the Sacred Tree: Black Women, Nature and Political

Resistance in Alice Walker's *Meridian*." In *Shifting the Ground: American Women Writers' Revision of Nature, Gender and Race*. Charlottesville: University of Virginia Press, 1997. 84–113.

Stepto, Robert B. *From Beyond the Veil: A Study of Afro-American Narrative*. Chicago: University of Illinois Press, 1991.

Strong-Leek, Linda M. "Excising the Spiritual, Physical and Psychological Self: An Analysis of Female Circumcision in the Works of Flora Nwapa, Ngugi wa Thiong'o and Alice Walker." Ph.D. diss., Michigan State University, 1994.

Thiam, Awa. *Speak Out, Black Sisters: Feminism and Oppression in Black Africa*. London: Pluto, 1978.

Thompson, R. W. *Black Caribbean*. London: Macdonald, 1946.

Trinh T. Min-ha. *Woman Native Other: Writing Postcoloniality and Feminism*. Bloomington: Indiana University Press, 1989.

Umeh, Marie. "Reintegration with the Lost Self: A Study of Buchi Emecheta's *Double Yoke*." In *Ngambika: Studies of Women in African Literature*. Eds. Carole B. Davies and Anne Adams Graves. Trenton, N.J.: Africa World Press, 1986. 173–80.

Vincent, Theo. *Seventeen Black and African Writers on Literature and Life*. Lagos: Cross Continent Press, 1981.

Vrettos, Athena. "Curative Domains: Women, Healing and History in Black Women's Narratives." *Women's Studies* 16, no. 4 (1989): 455–73.

Walcott, Derek. *In a Green Night*. London: Jonathan Cape, 1962.

Walker, Alice. *By the Light of My Father's Smile*. New York: Random House, 1998.

———. *The Color Purple*. New York: Washington Square, 1983.

———. "Everyday Use." In *In Love and Trouble: Stories of Black Women*. New York: Harcourt Brace Jovanovich, 1973.

———. *In Search of Our Mothers' Gardens: Womanist Prose*. New York: Harcourt Brace Jovanovich, 1983.

———. "Karamojans." In *Once*. New York: Harcourt, Brace and World, 1968. 20–24.

———. *Living by the Word*. New York: Harcourt, Brace, Jovanovich, 1988.

———. "Looking for Zora." In *I Love Myself When I Am Laughing . . . And Then Again When I Am Looking Mean and Impressive*. Old Westbury, N.Y.: Feminist Press, 1979. 297–313.

———. *Meridian*. New York: Pocket Books, 1986.

———. *Possessing the Secret of Joy*. New York: Pocket Books, 1992.

———. *The Temple of My Familiar*. New York: Harcourt, Brace, Jovanovich, 1989.

———. *Warrior Marks: Female Genital Mutilation and the Sexual Blinding of Women*. New York: Harcourt, Brace, 1993.

Walters, Ron. *Pan Africanism in the African Diaspora: The African American Linkage*. Detroit, Mich.: Wayne State University Press, 1991.

Watson, Steven. *The Harlem Renaissance: Hub of African American Culture, 1920–1930*. New York: Pantheon, 1995.

West, Cornel. "The New Cultural Politics of Difference." *October* 53 (1990): 93–109.

White, Evelyn. "Alice Walker on Finding Your Bliss." *Ms.* (September/October 1998): 44–50.

White, Hayden. *Tropics of Discourse: Essays in Cultural Criticism*. Baltimore, Md.: Johns Hopkins University Press, 1991.

Wilentz, Gay. *Binding Cultures: Black Women Writers in Africa and the Diaspora*. Bloomington: Indiana University Press, 1992.

———. "Mutilations of the Self." *The Women's Review of Books* 10, no. 5 (1993): 15–16.

———. "The Politics of Exile: Reflections of a Black-Eyed Squint in *Our Sister Killjoy.*" In *Emerging Perspectives on Ama Ata Aidoo.* Eds. Ada U. Azodo and Gay Wilentz. Trenton, N.J.: Africa World Press, 1999. 79–92.

Williams, John A. "Open Letter to an African." *Negro Digest* (September 1965): 22, 28–35.

Williams-Moen, Elizabeth. "Genital Mutilation: Everywoman's Problem." Working Paper #22 presented at the University of Colorado, Boulder, April 1993.

Wittig, Monique. "The Straight Mind." *Feminist Issues* 1 (1980): 103–12.

Wright, Bruce M. "The African Affair." In *American Negro Poetry.* Ed. Arna Bontemps. New York: Hill and Wang, 1974.

index